Symmetry Art Patterns.
coloring and design inspiration book

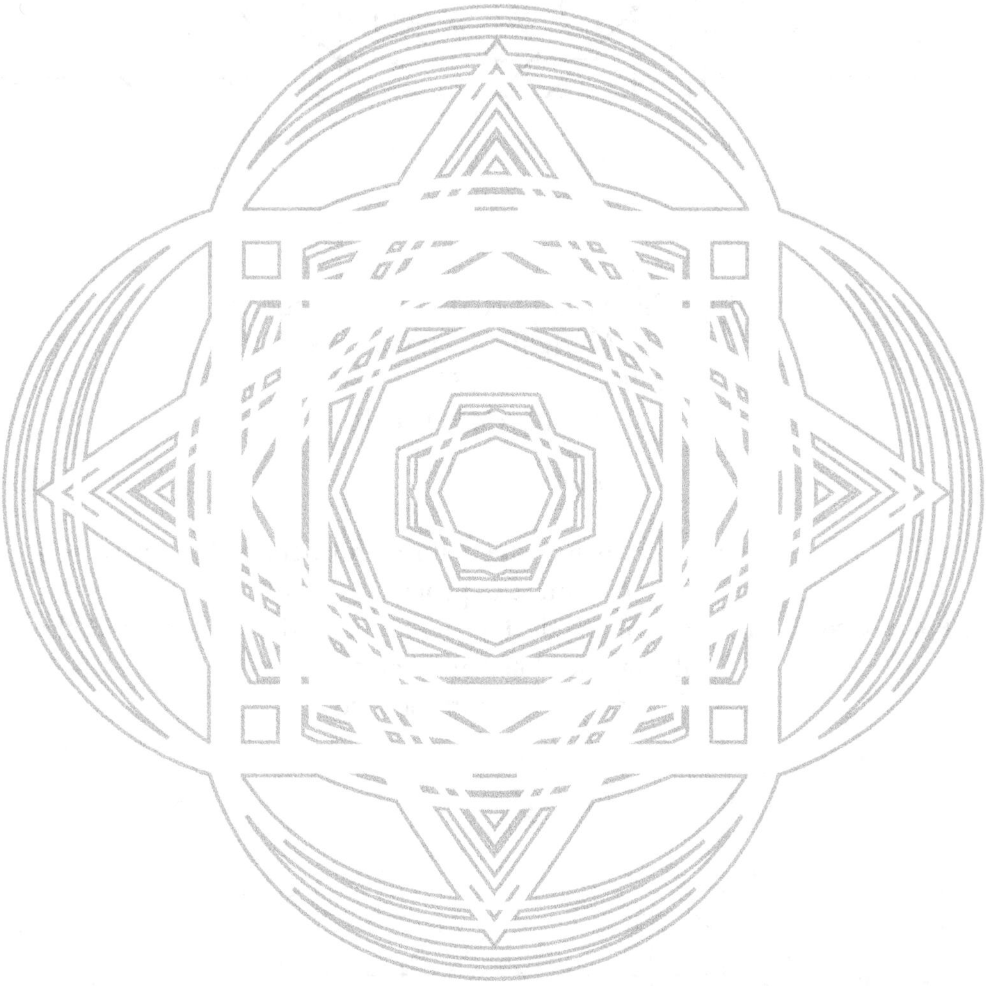

48 designs for coloring and inspiration

24 symmetrical design elements + 24 patterns
by
The Symmetry Masters

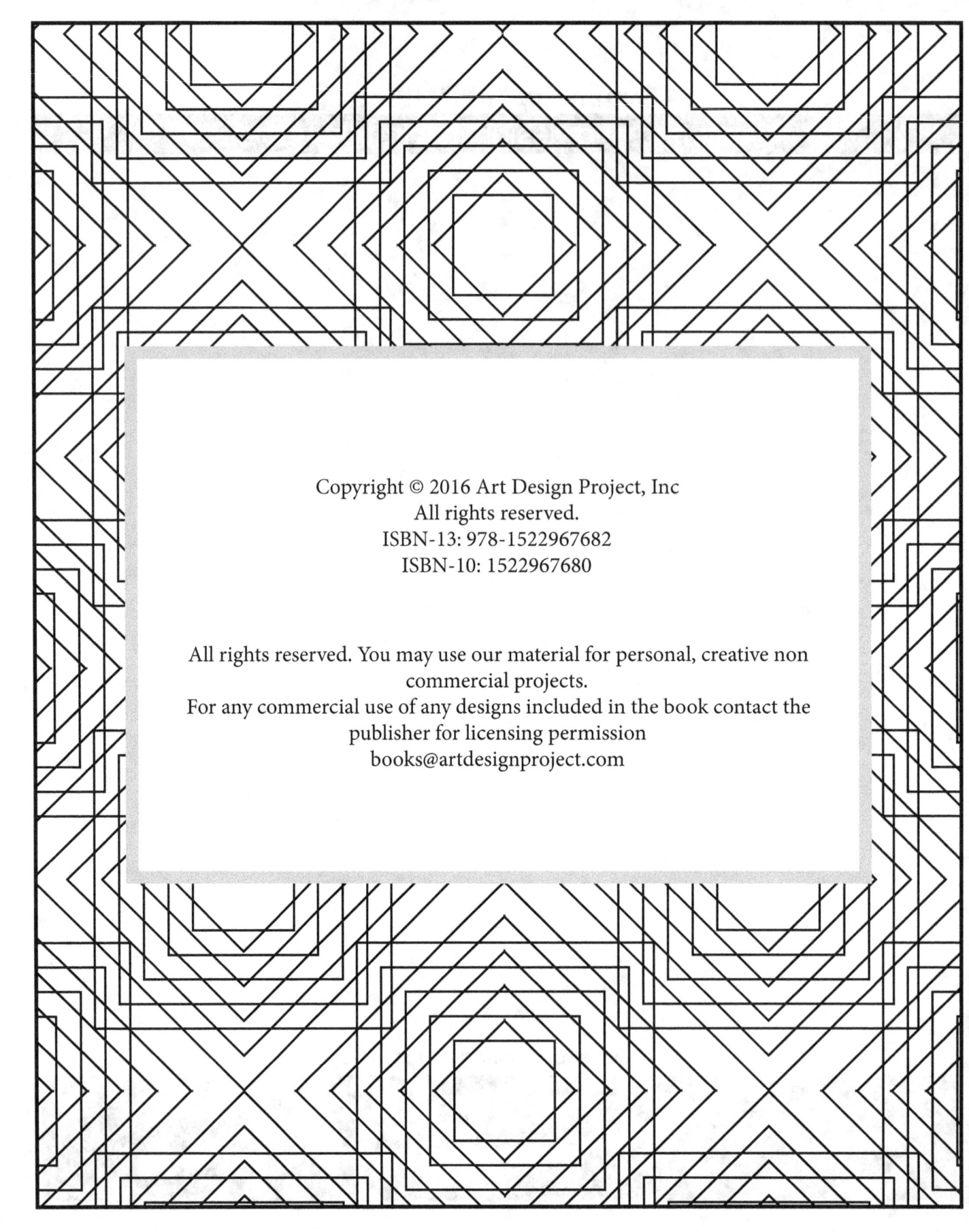

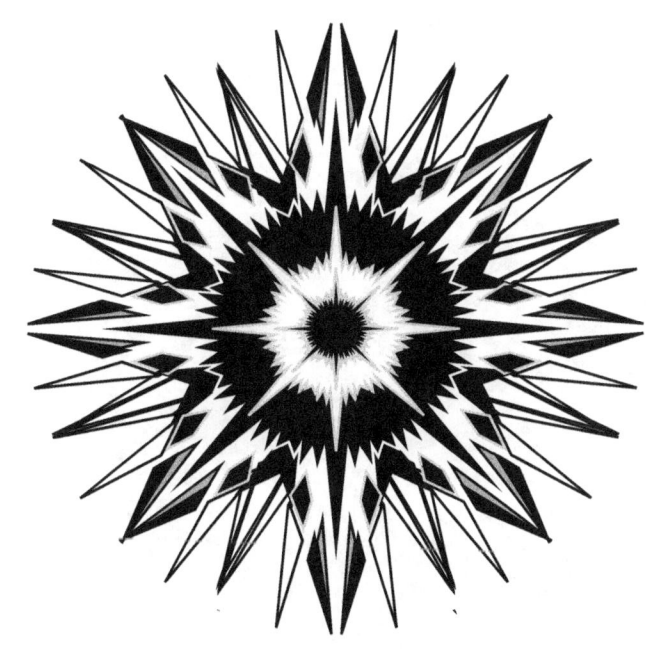

symmetry-art

By Symmetry Masters

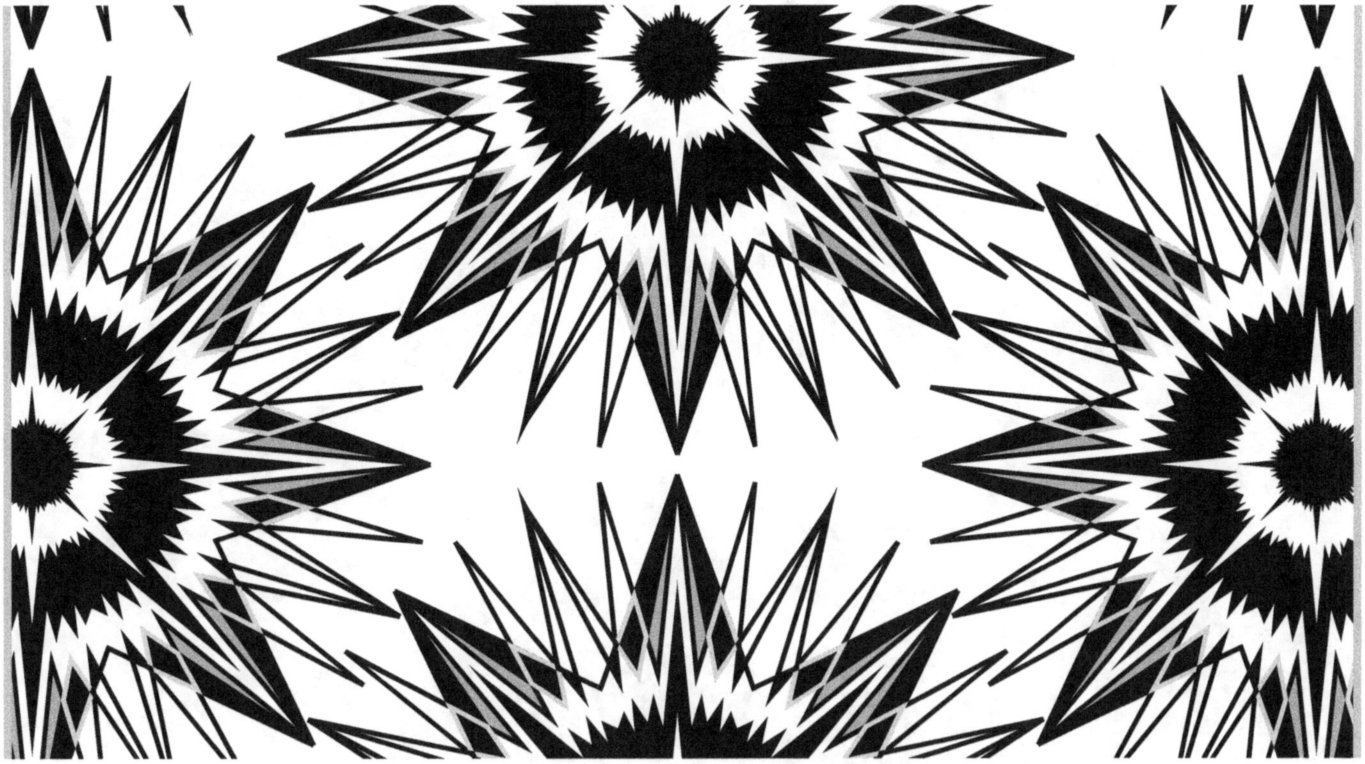

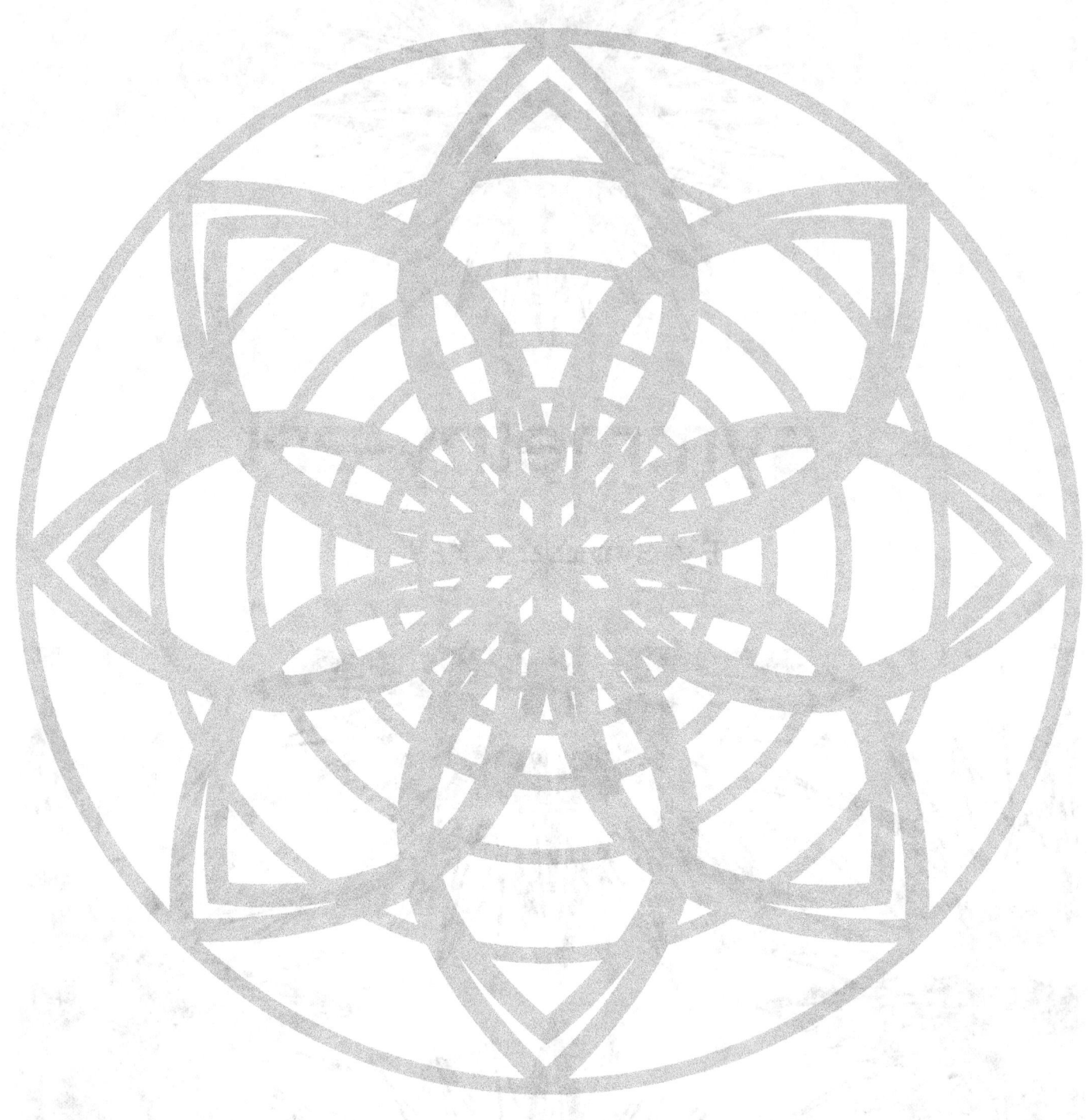

pattern # 1

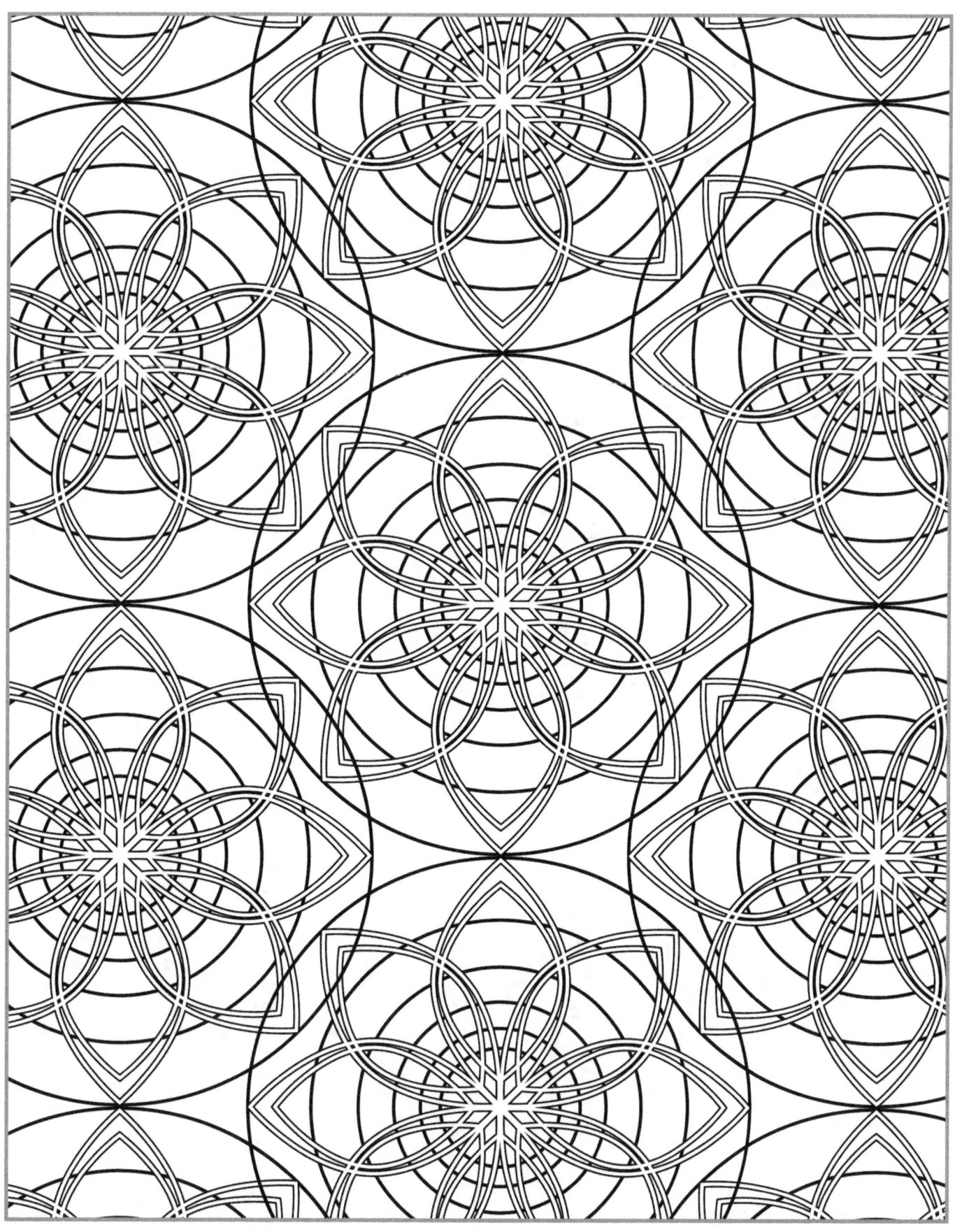

pattern # 2

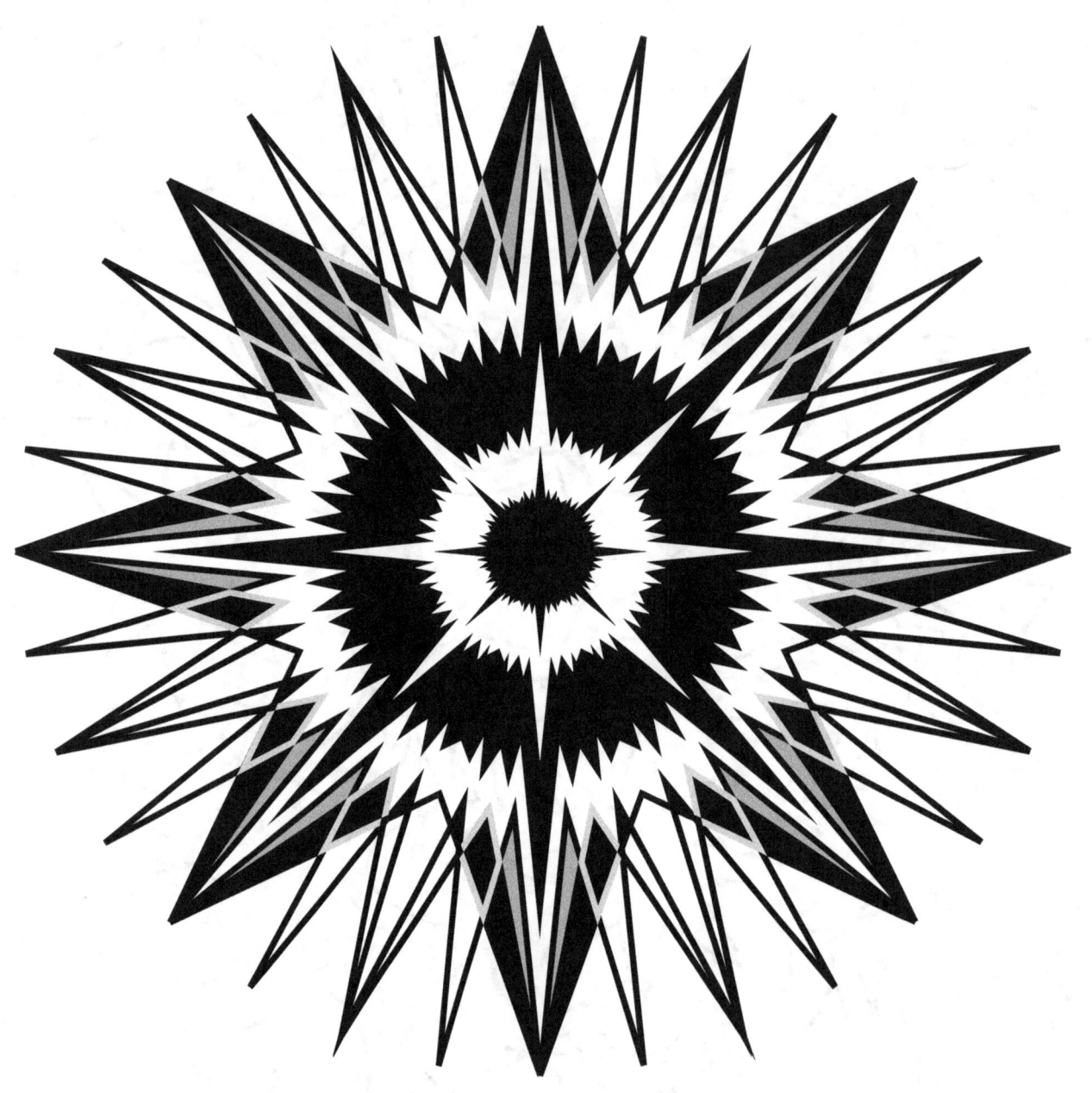

pattern # 3

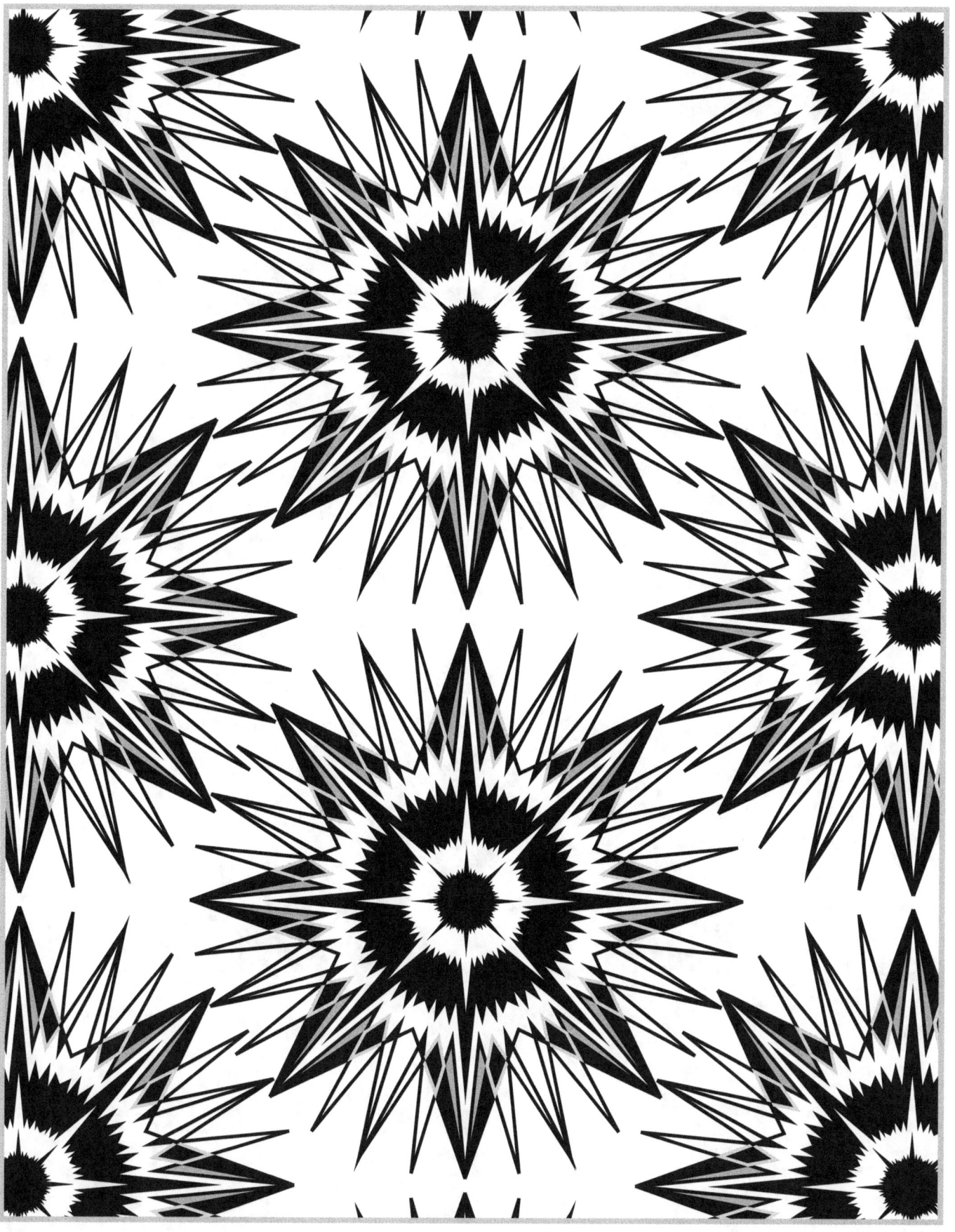

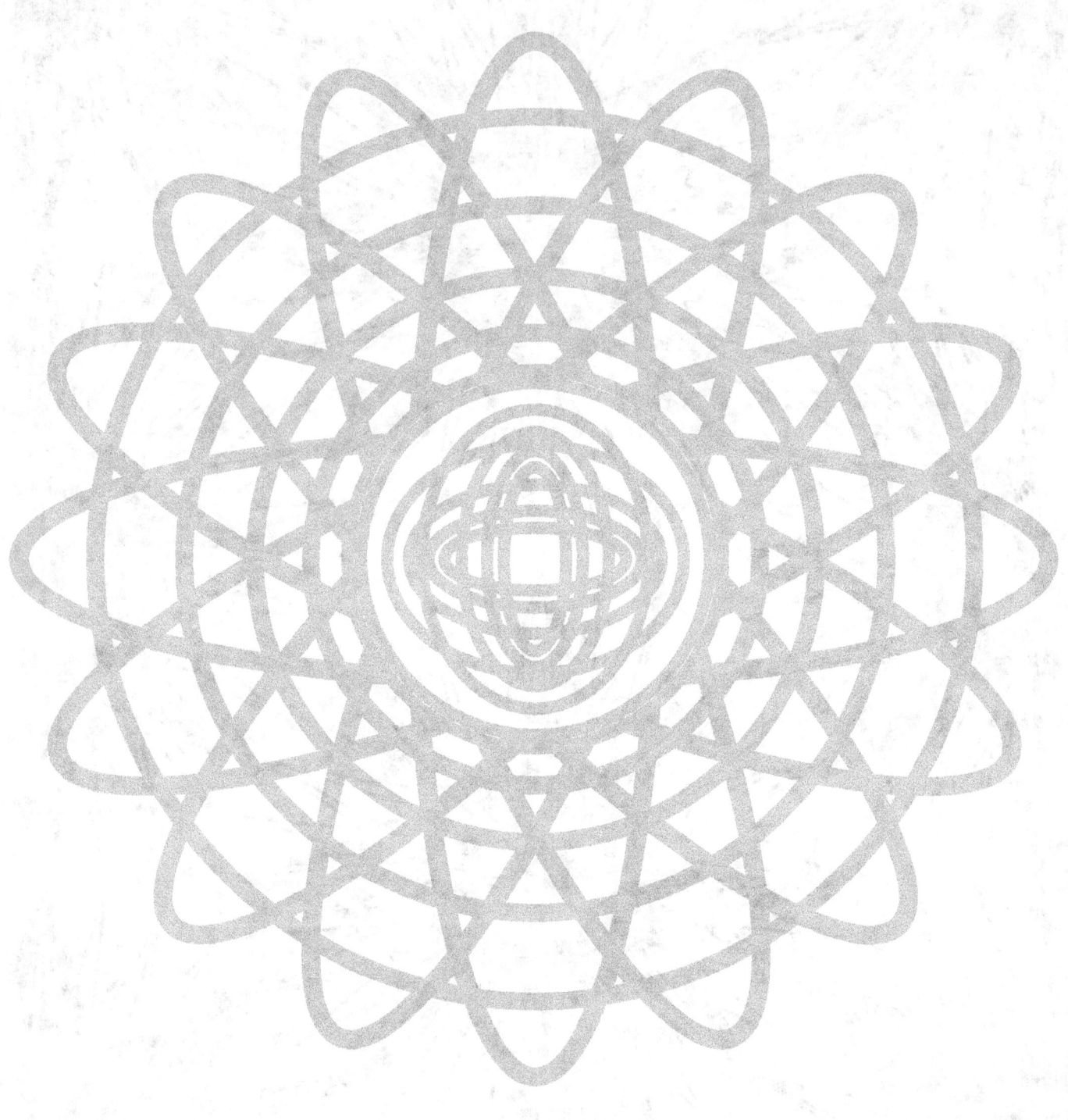

pattern # 4

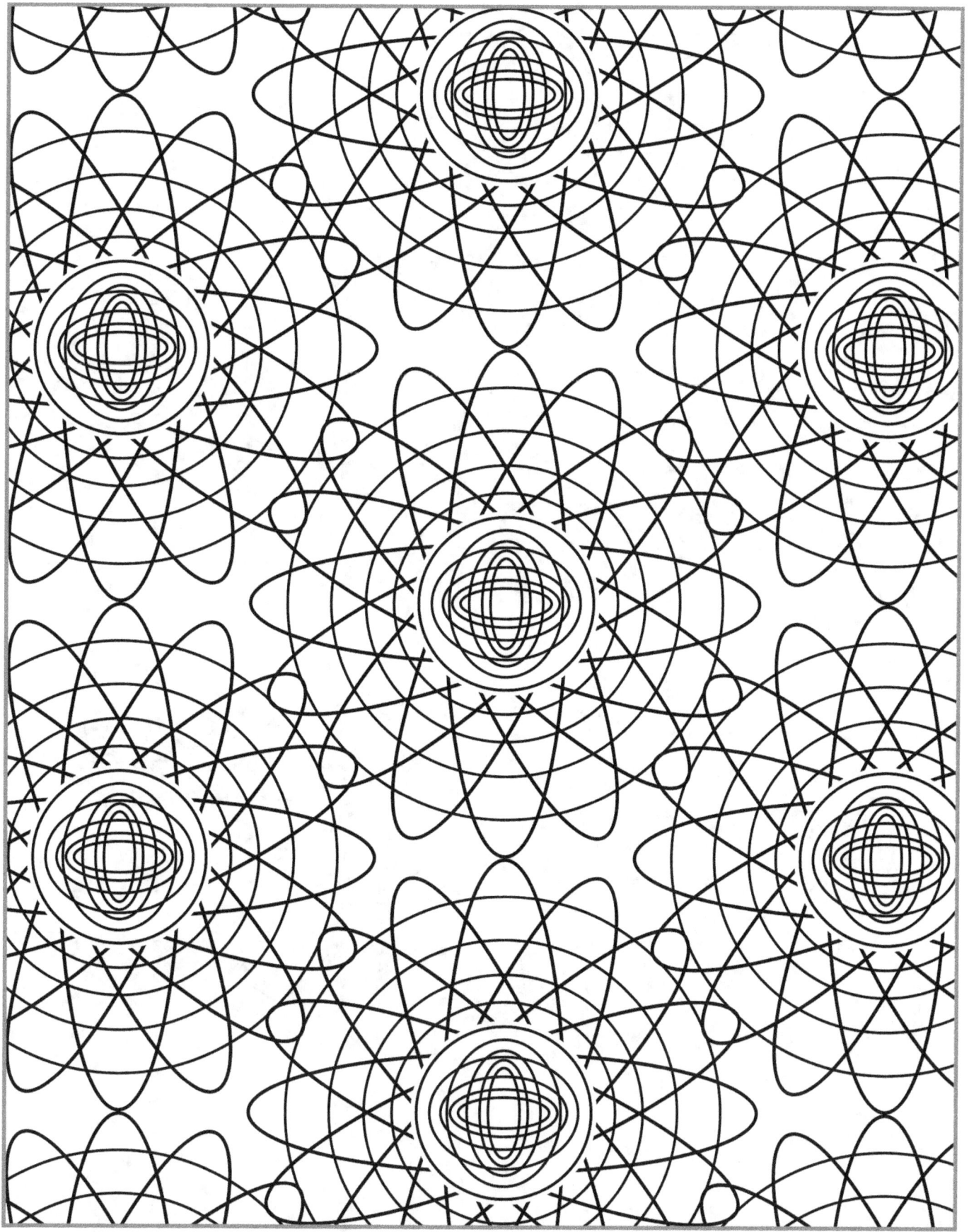

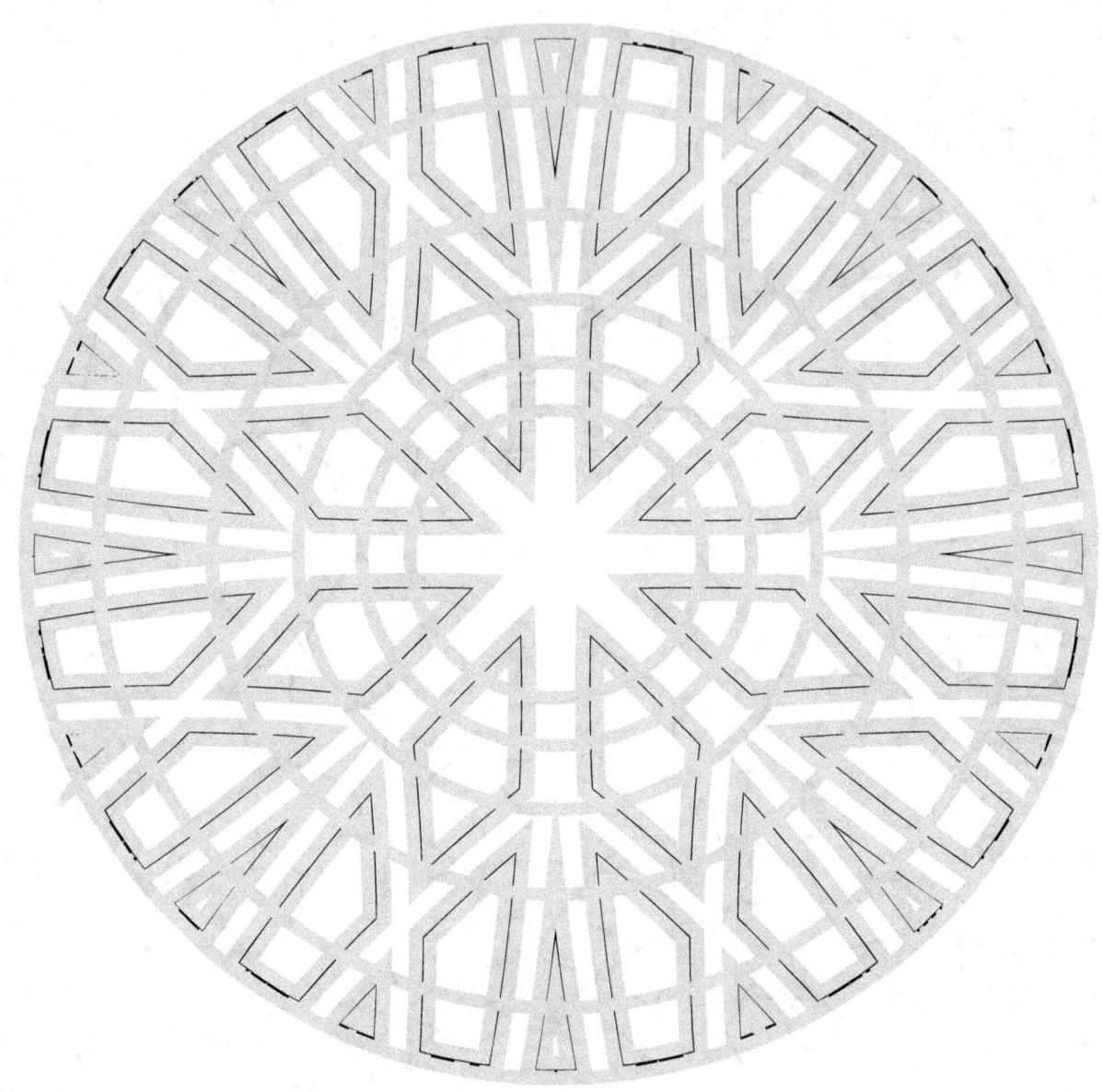

pattern # 5

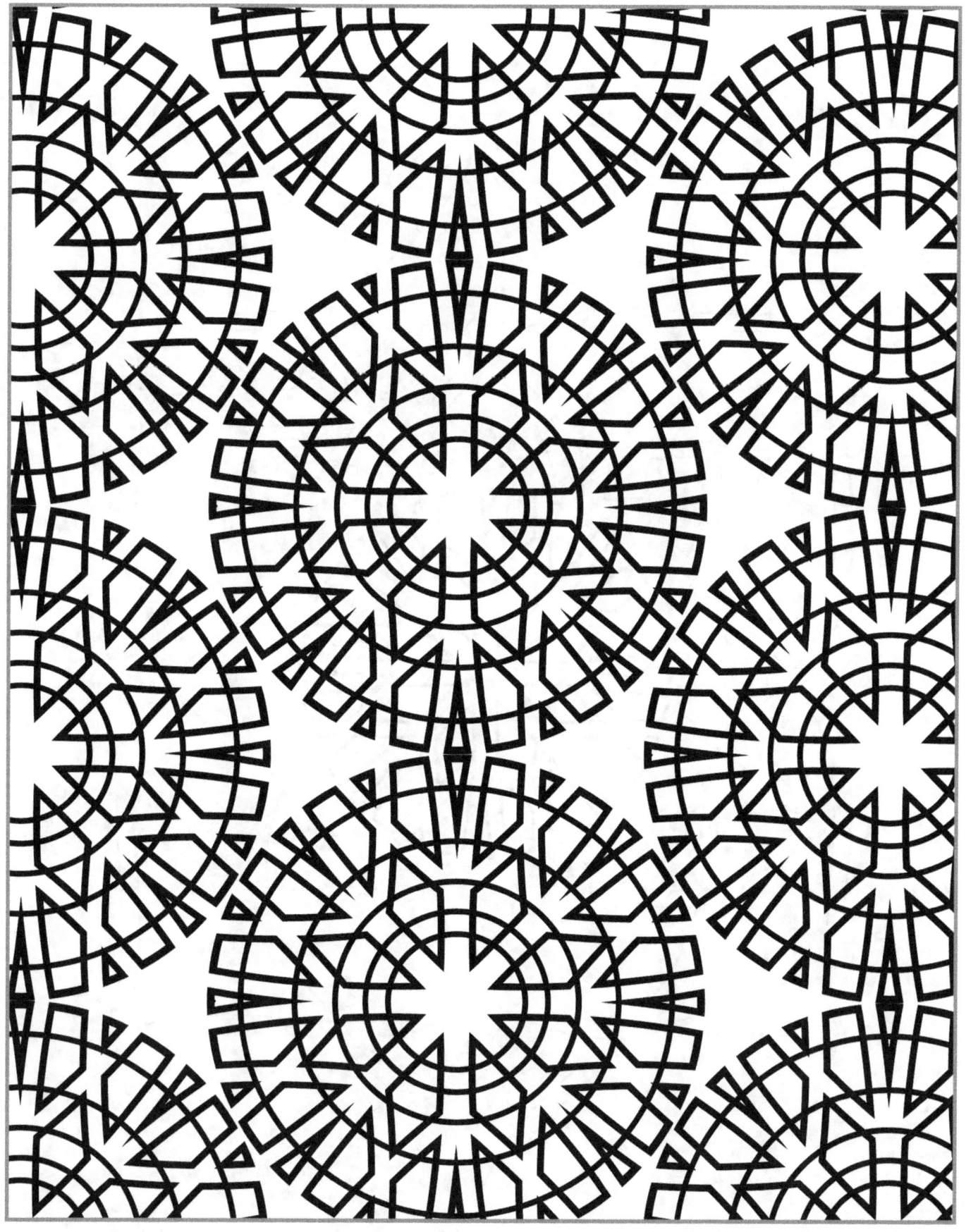

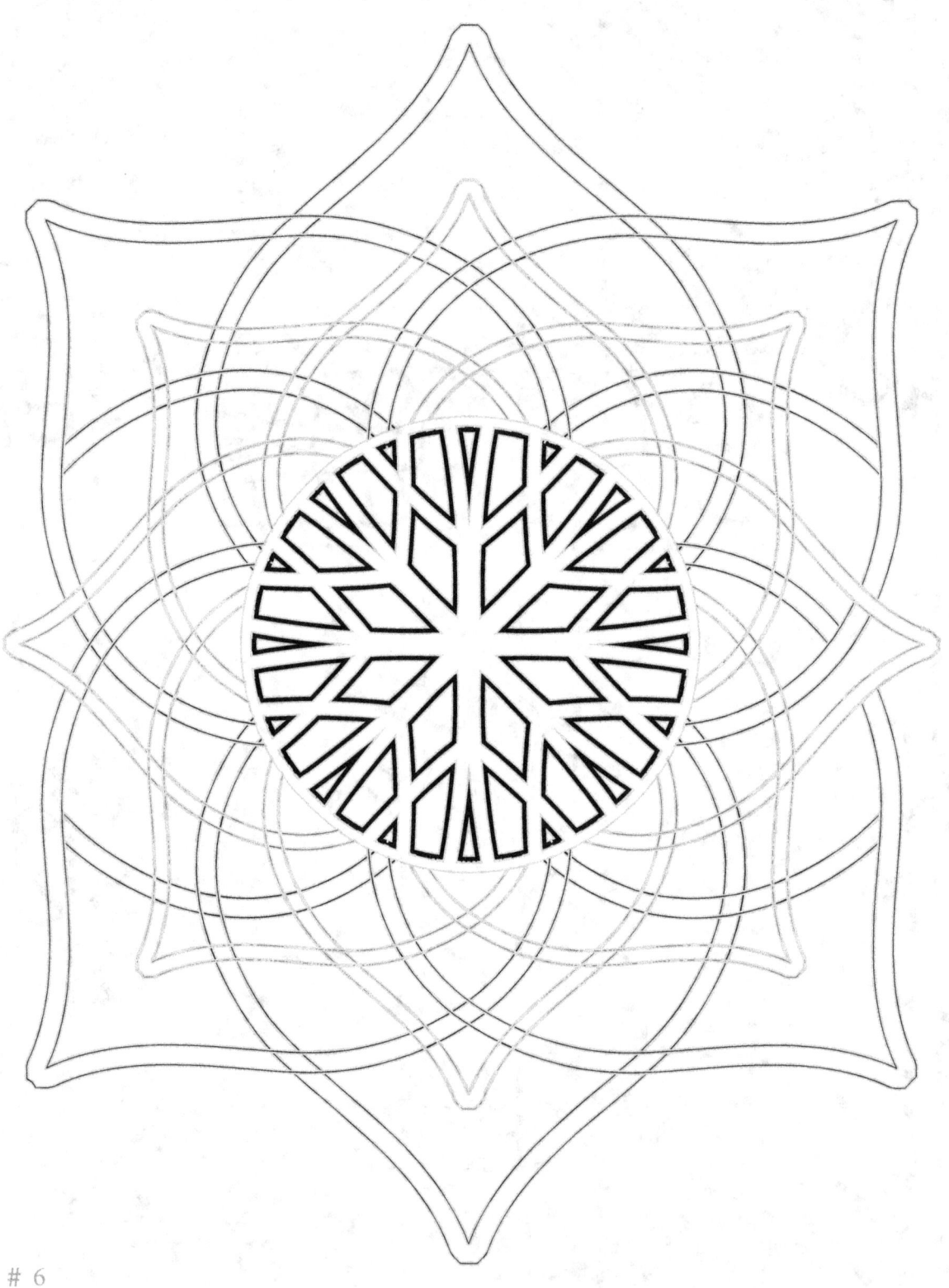

pattern # 6

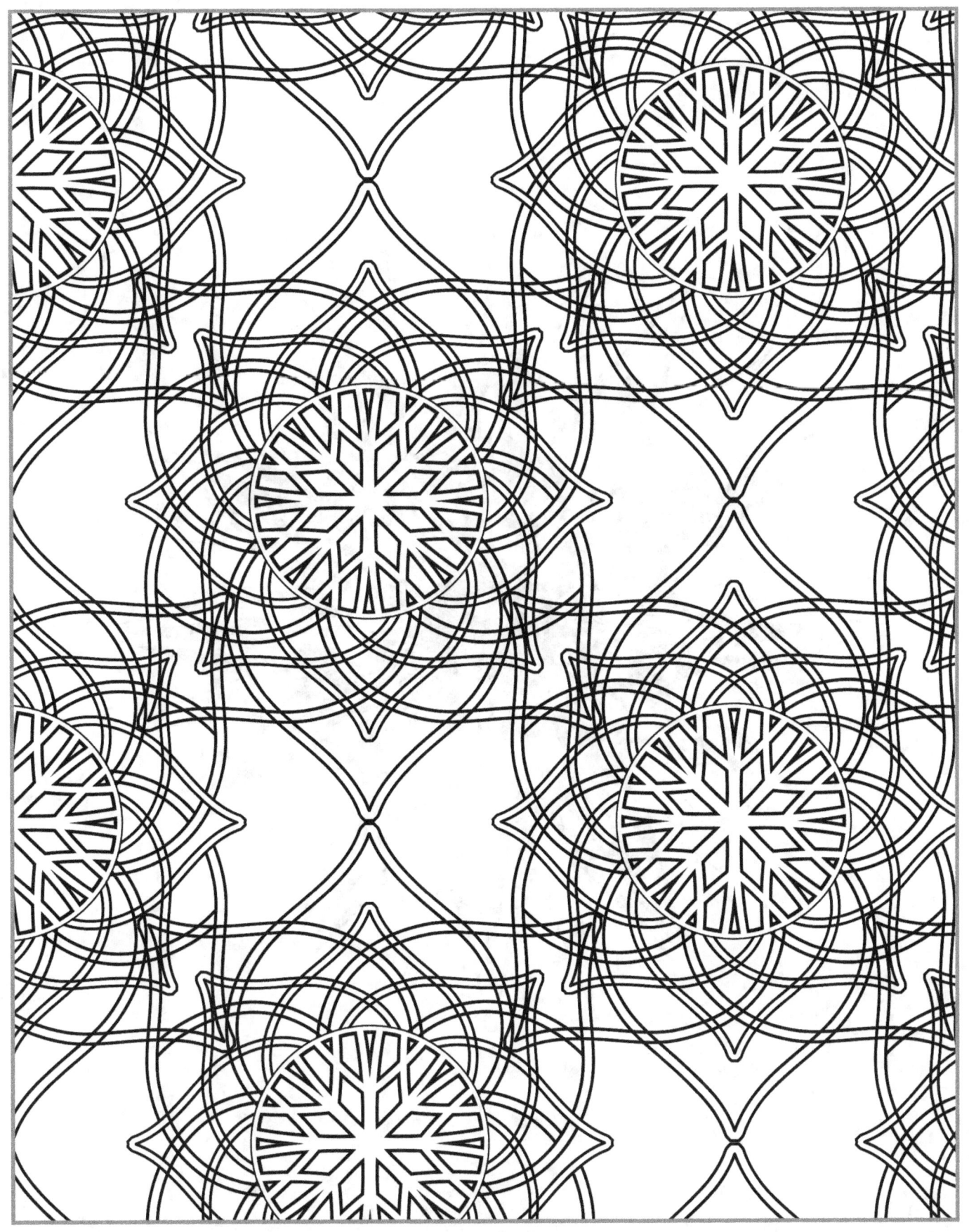

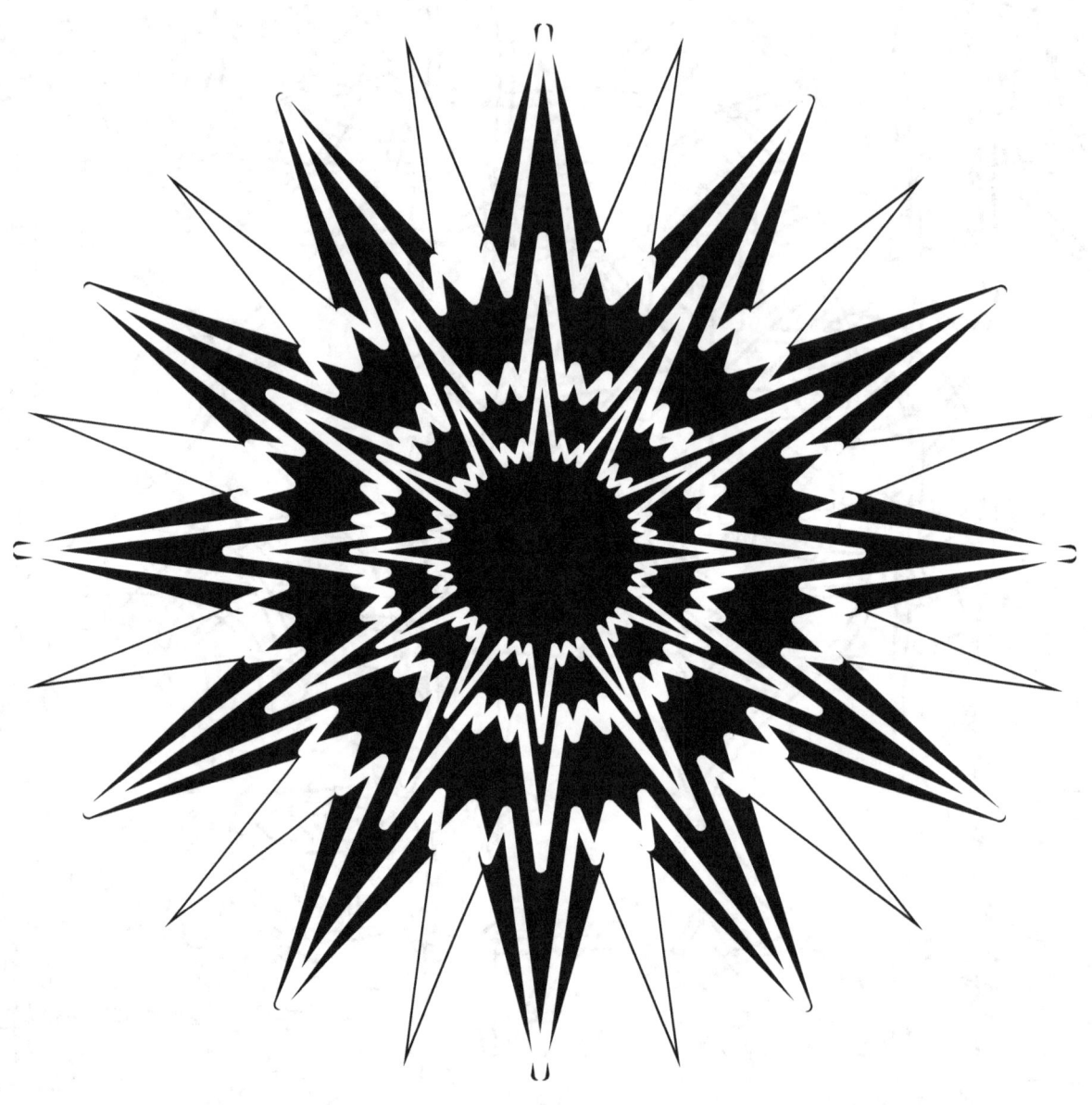

pattern # 7

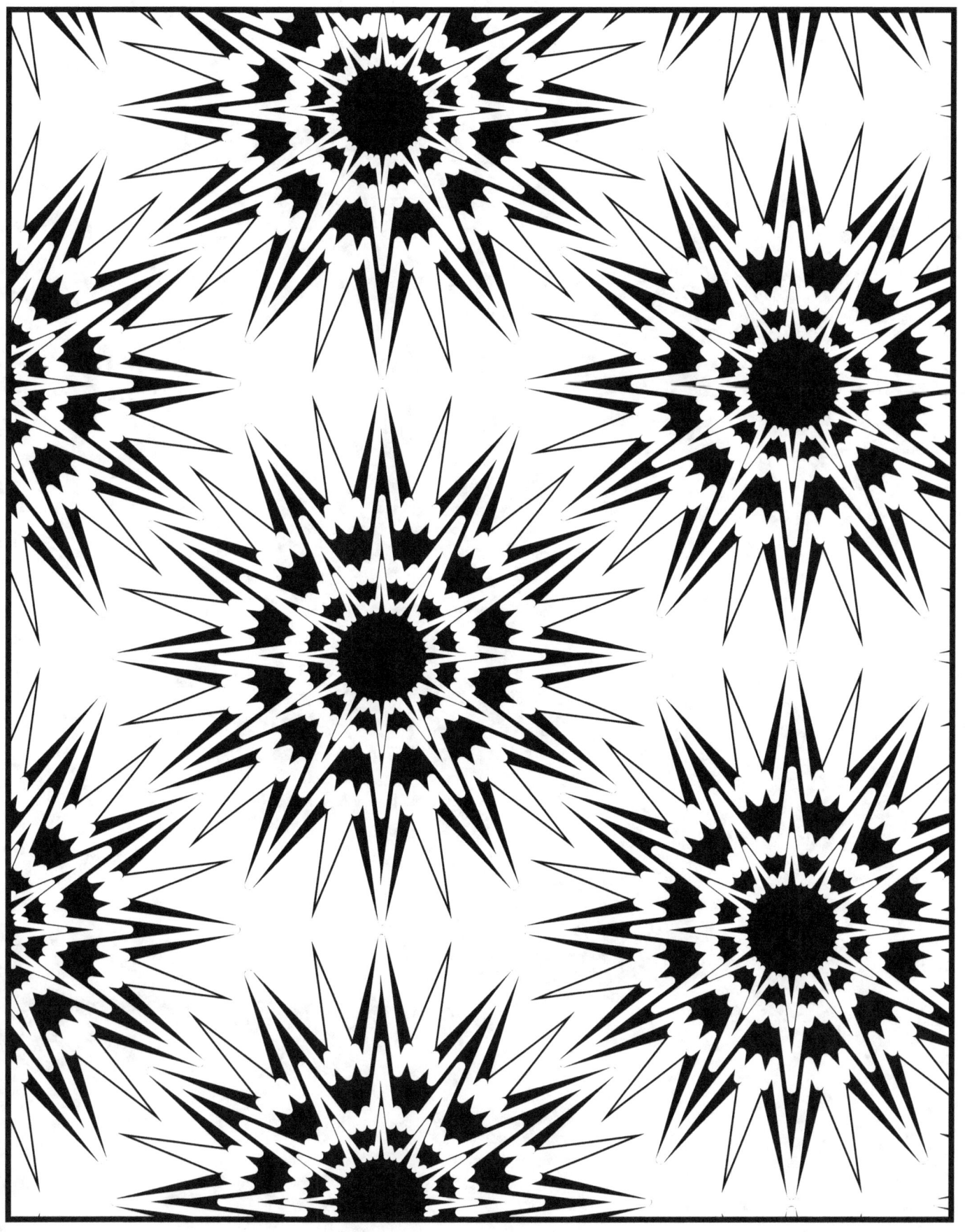

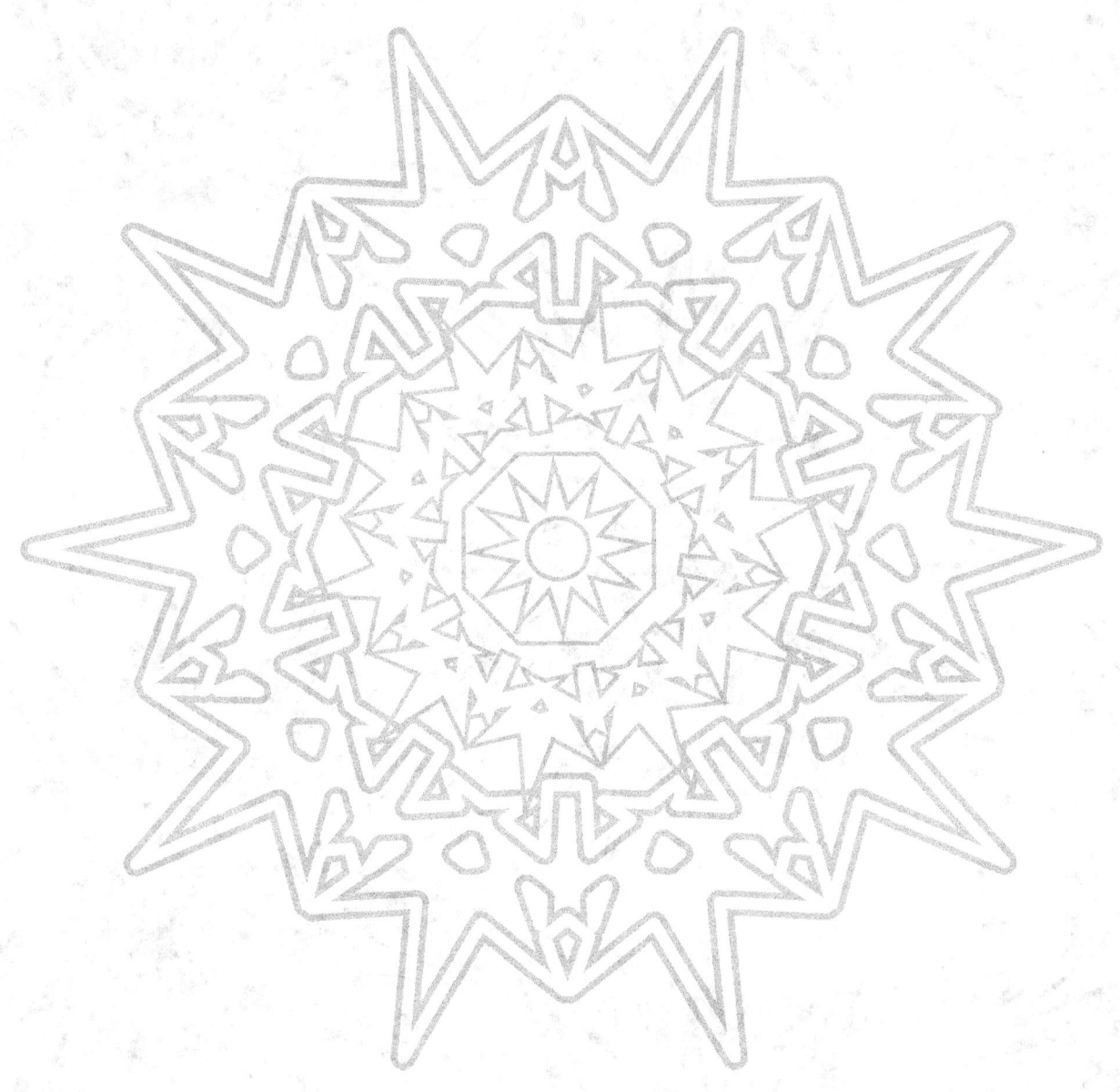

pattern # 8

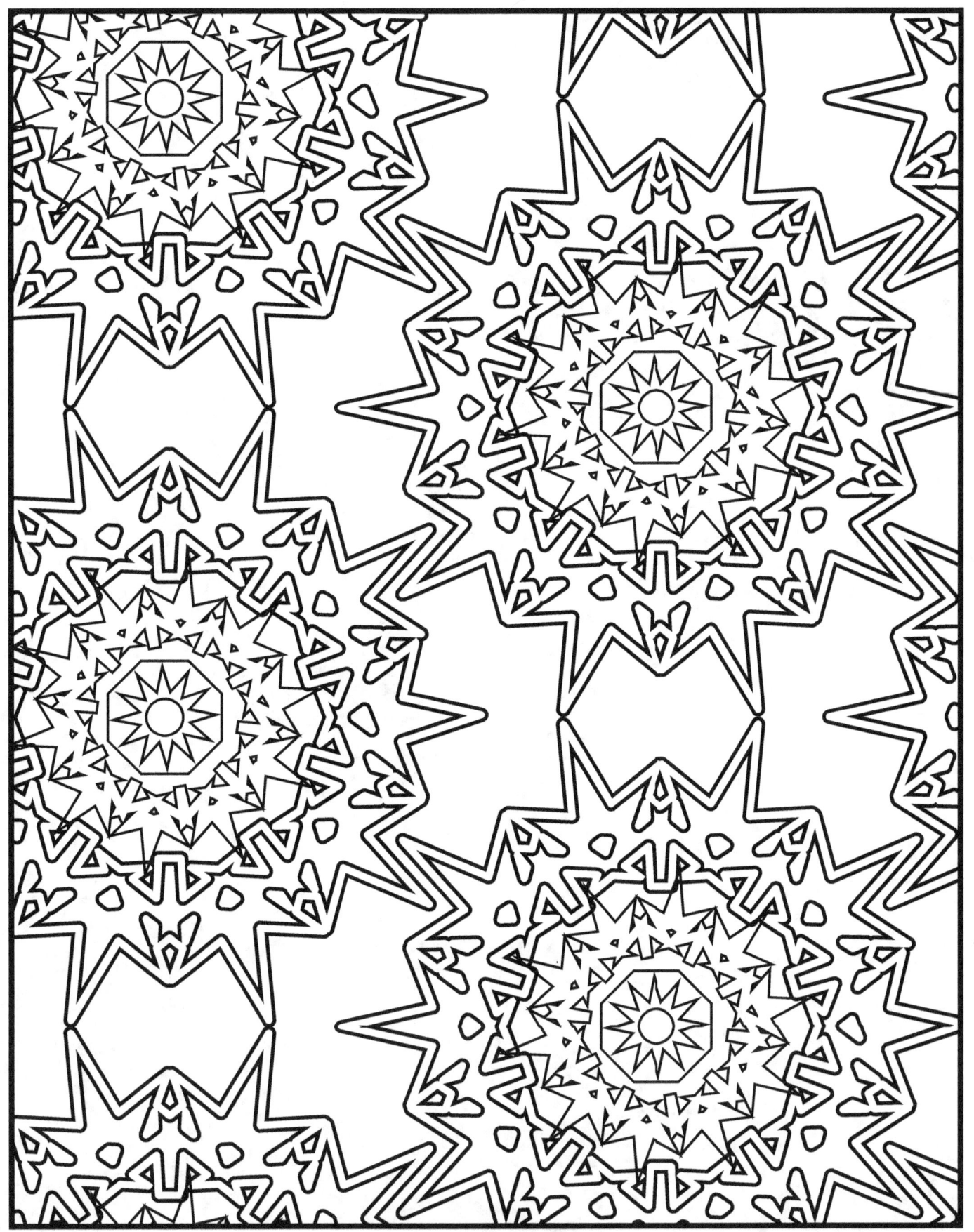

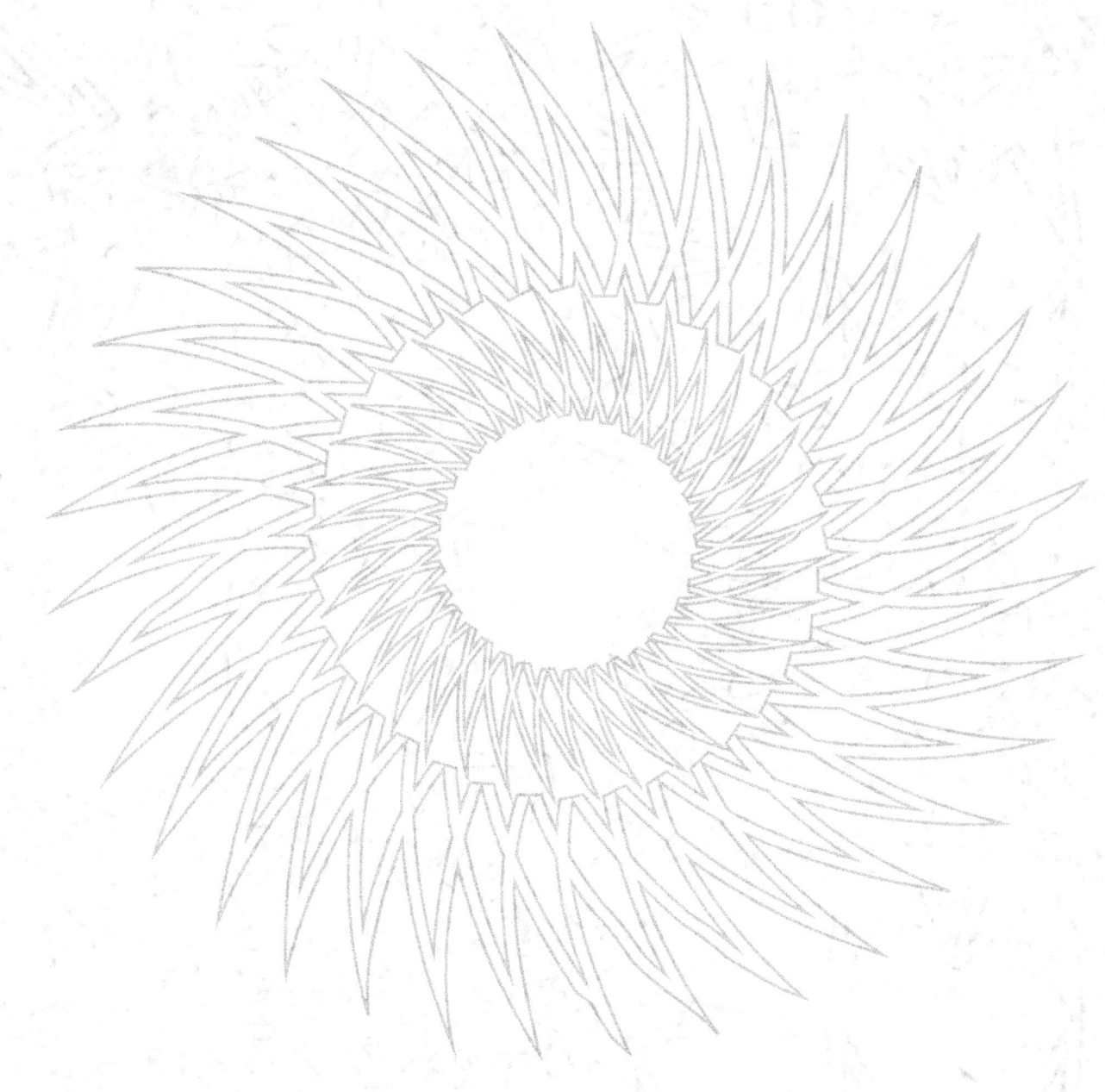

pattern # 9

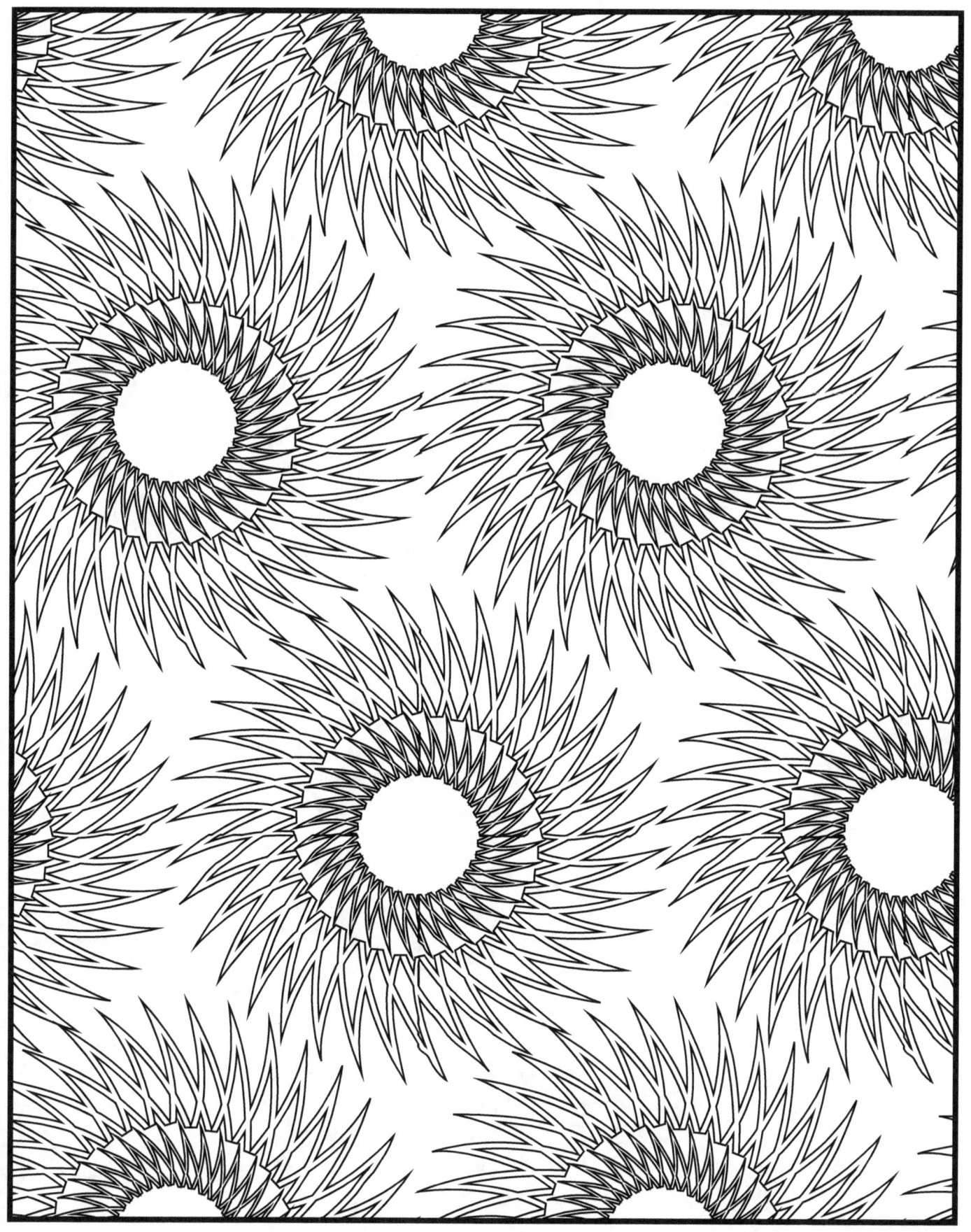

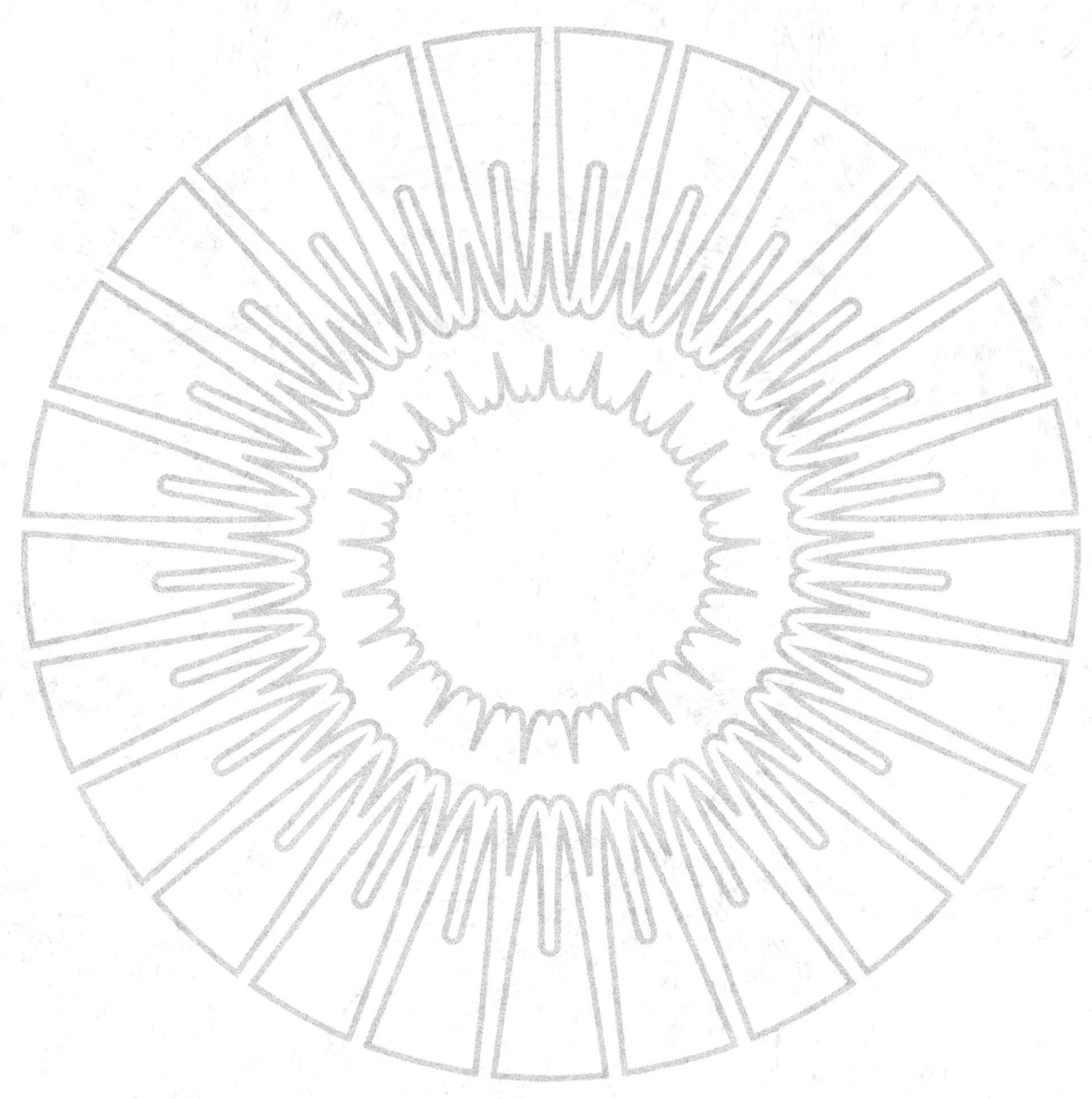

pattern # 10

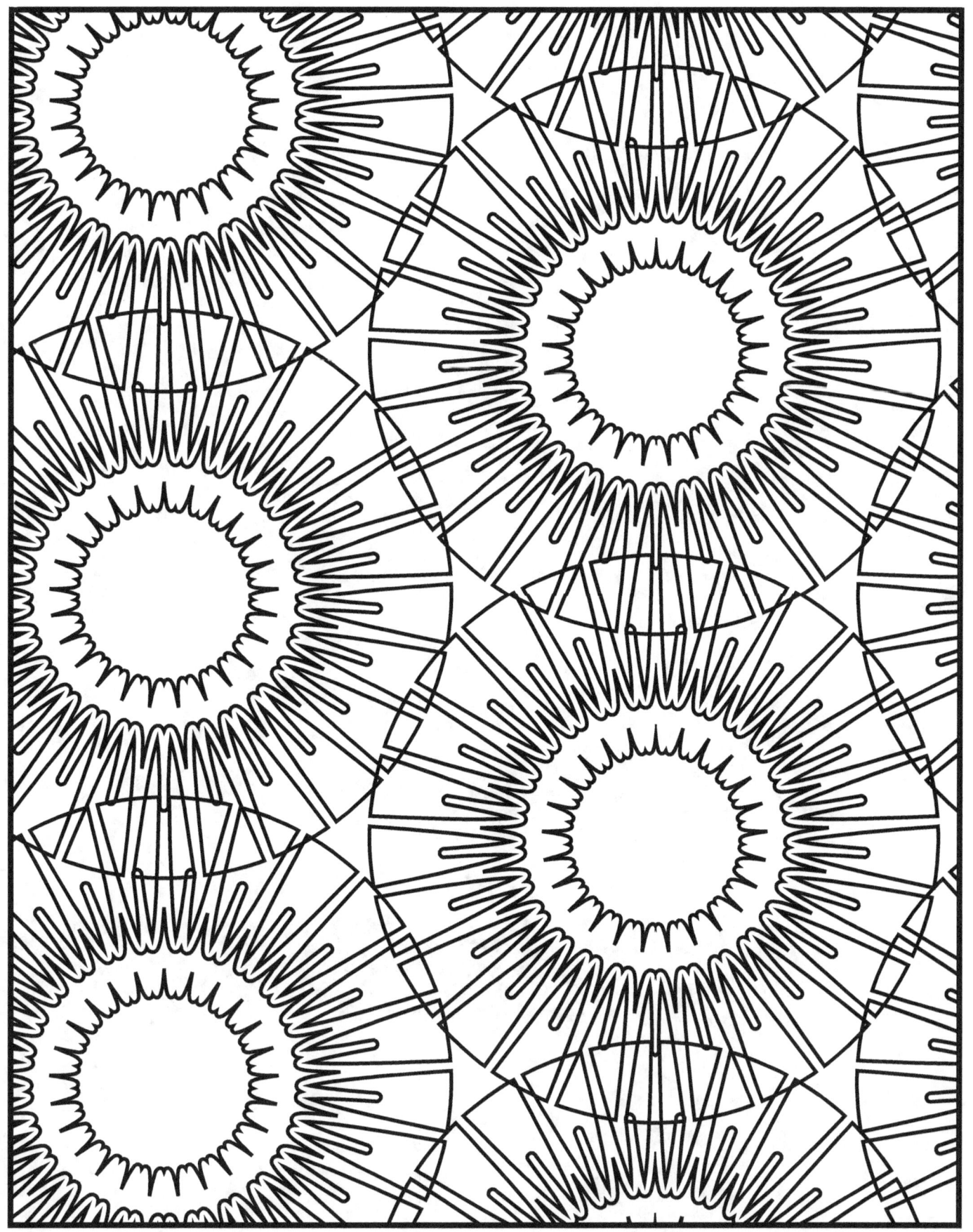

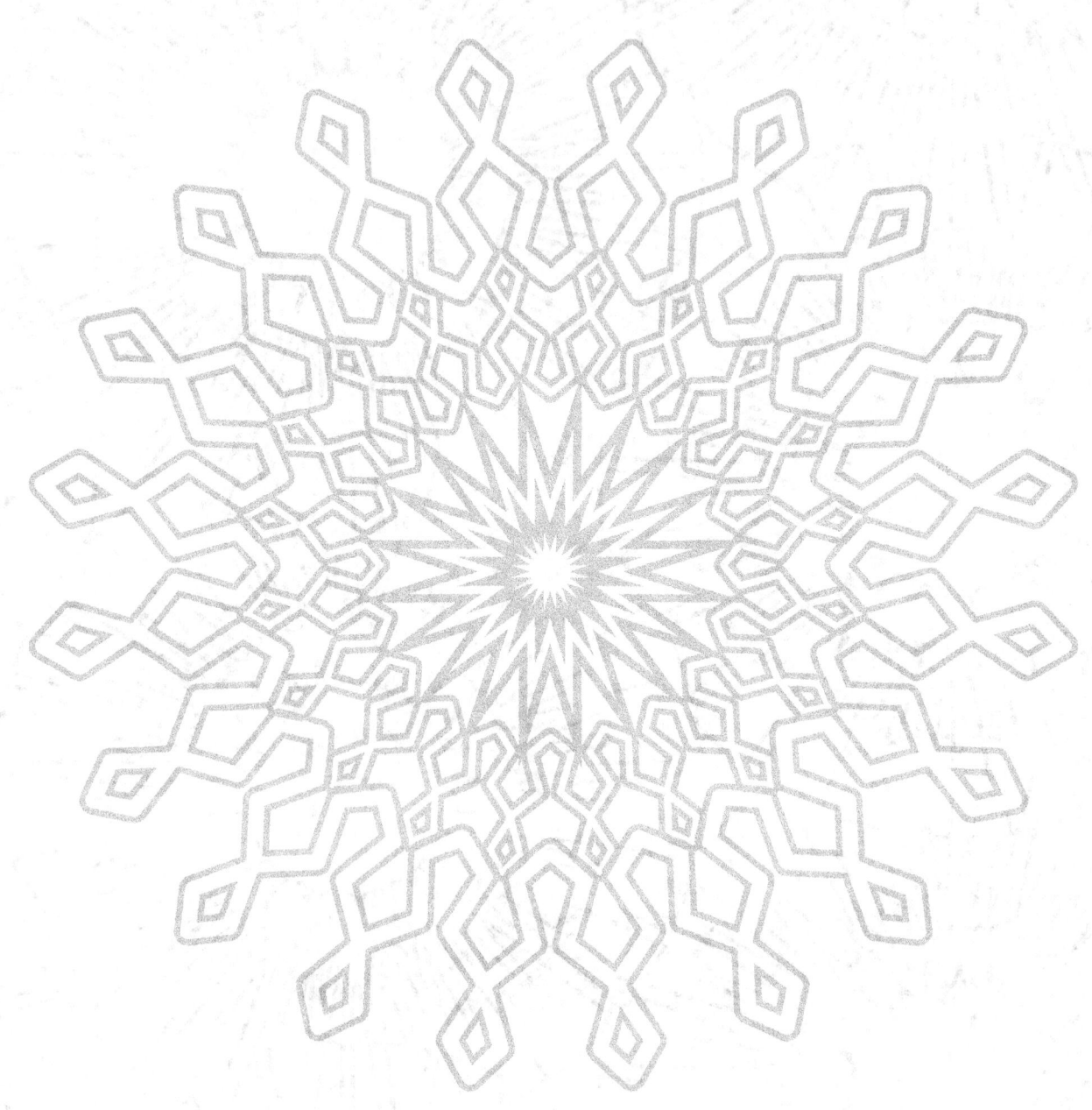

pattern # 11

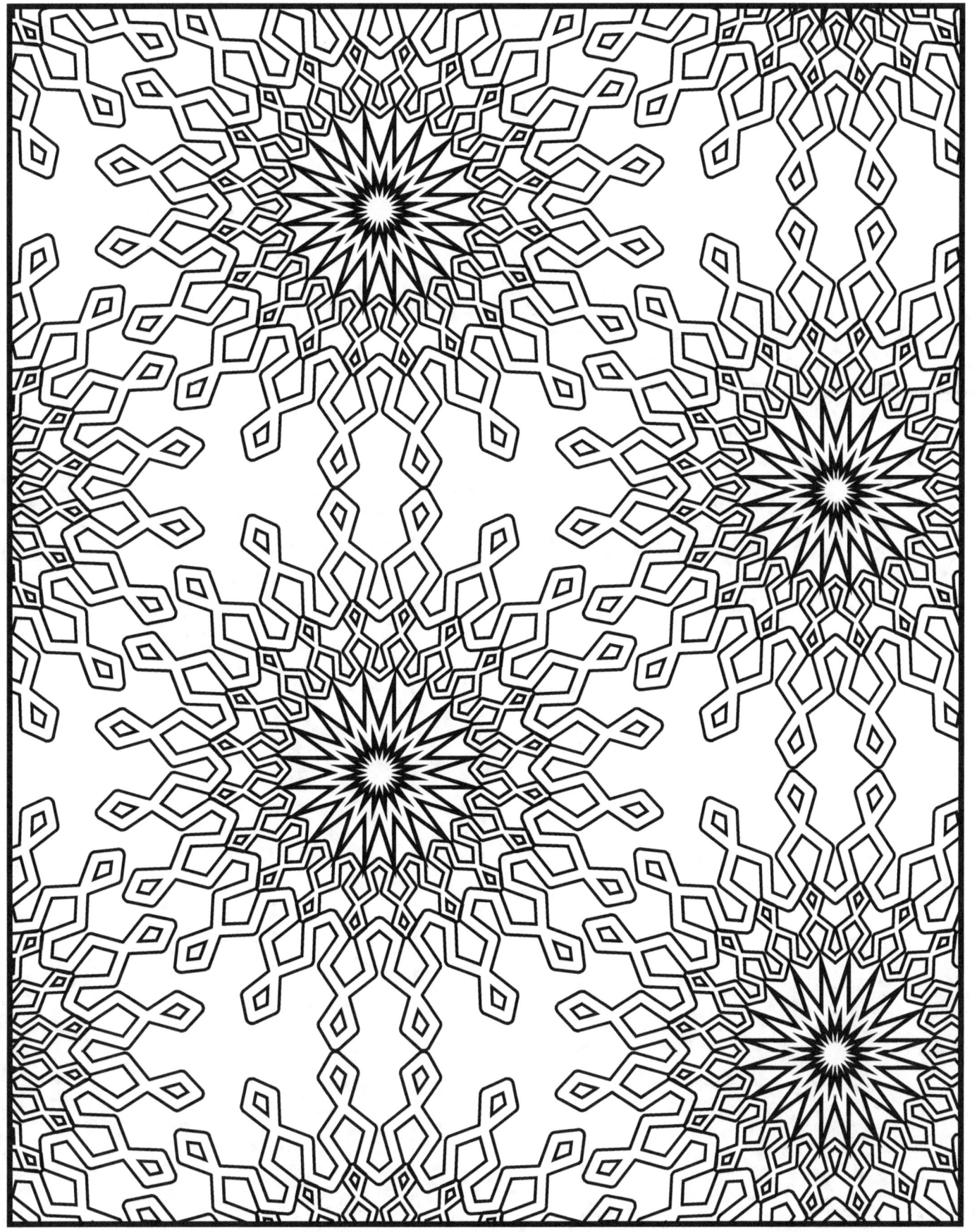

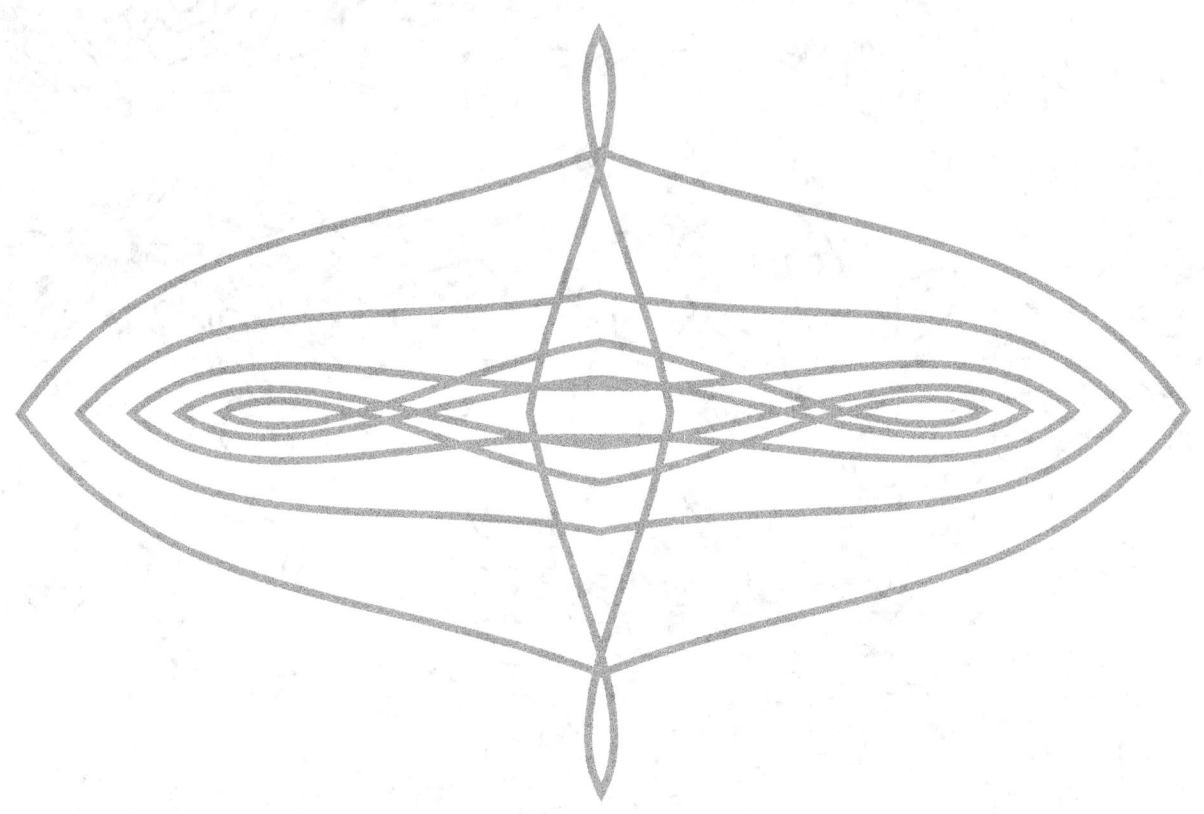

pattern # 12

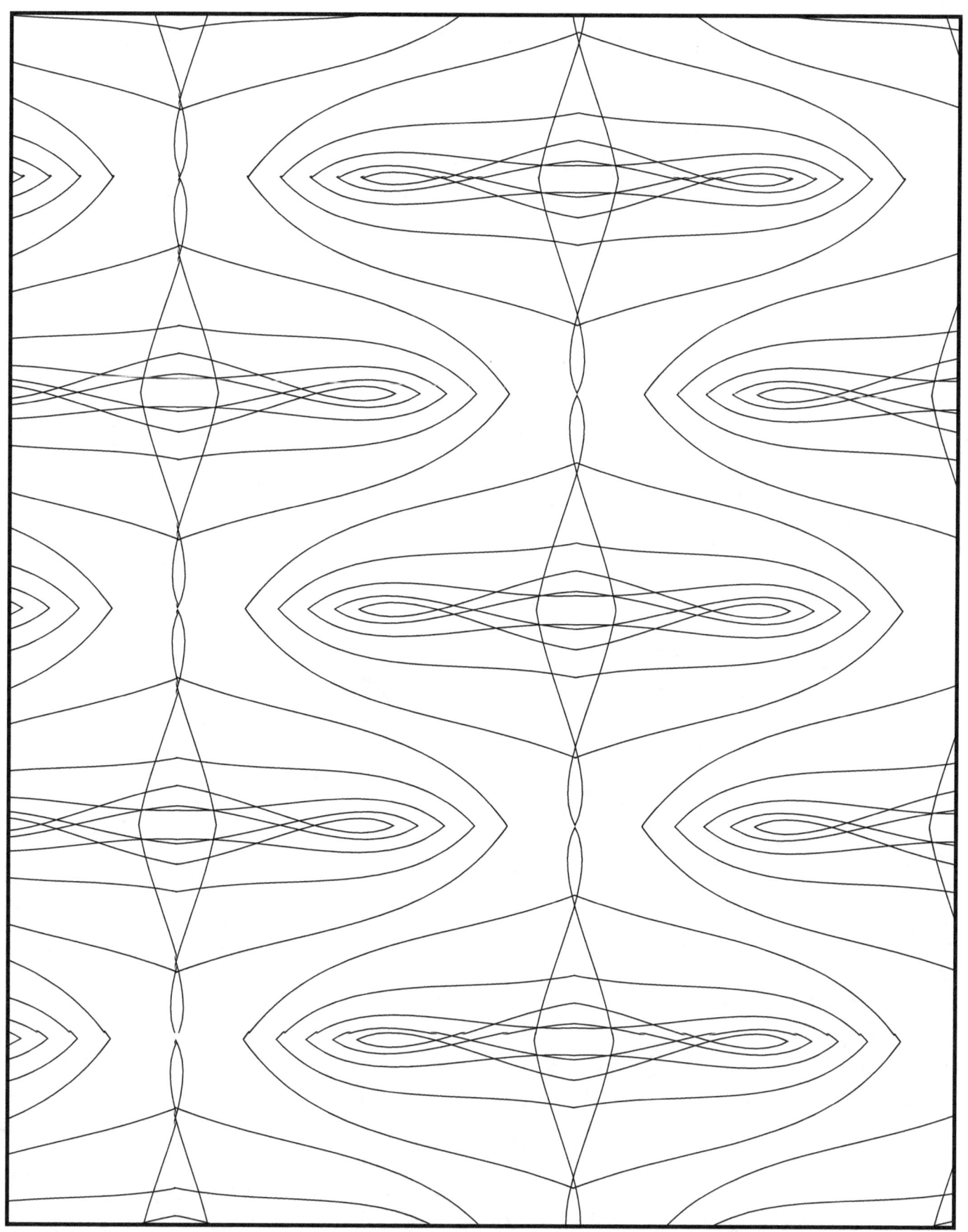

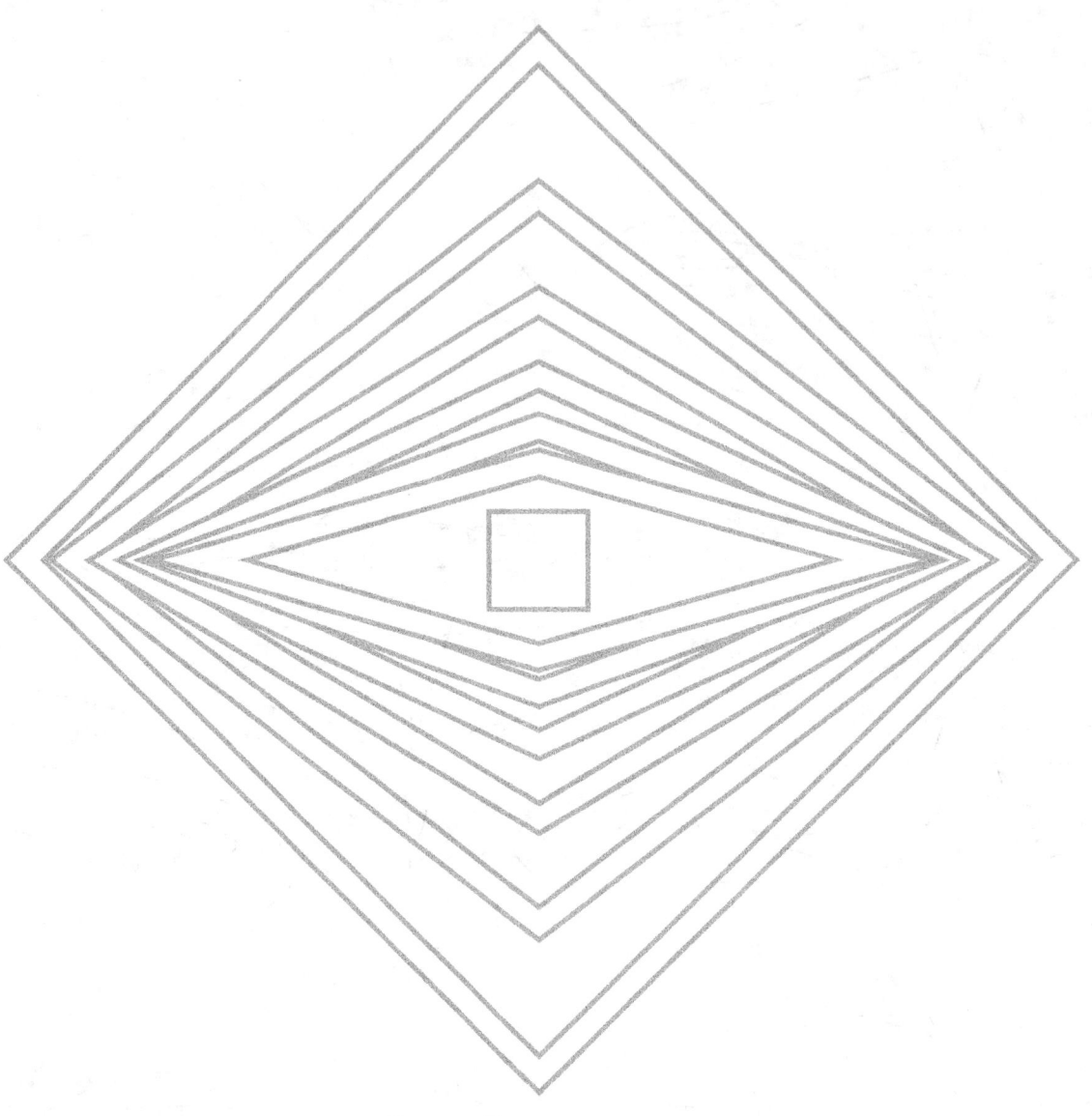

pattern # 13

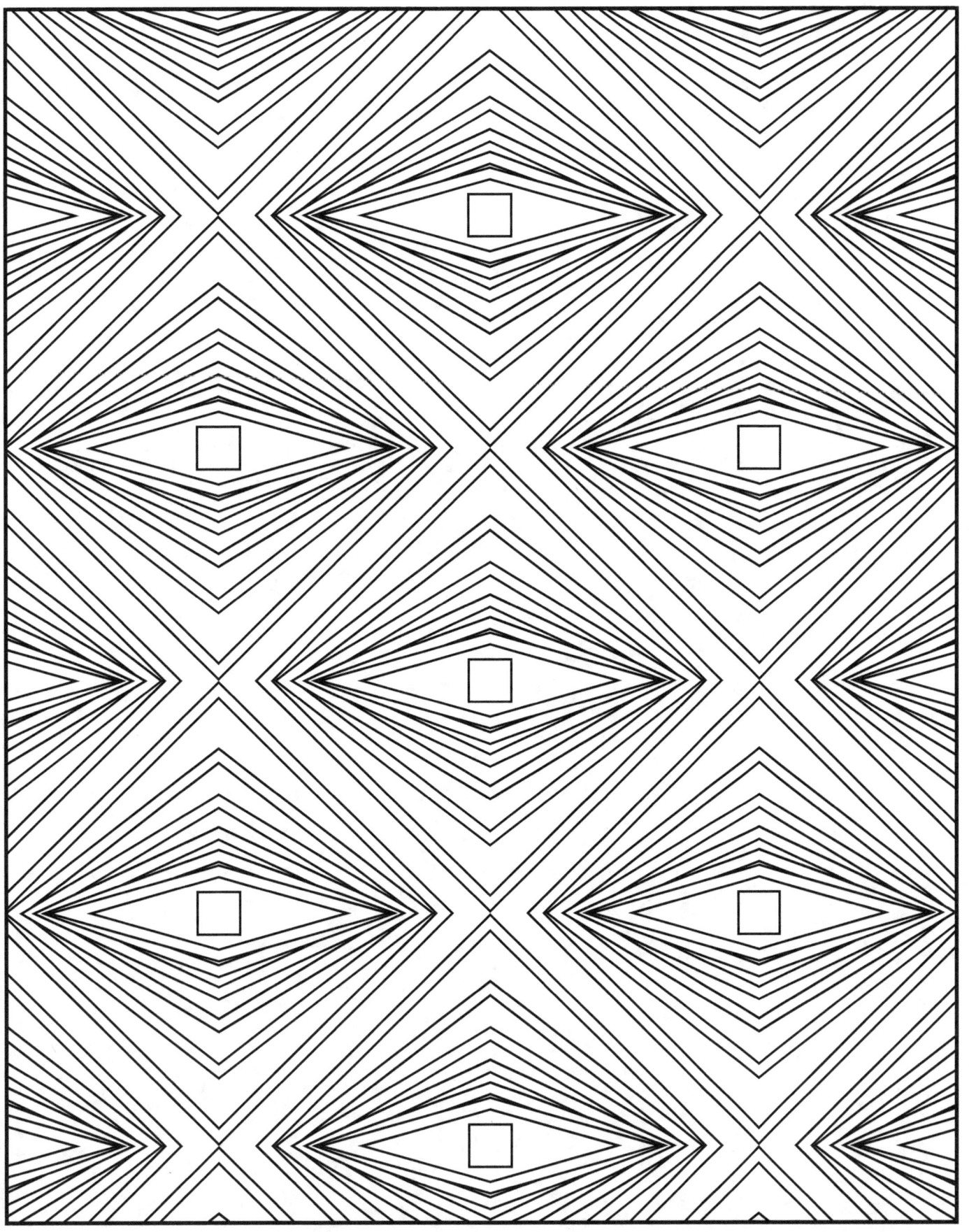

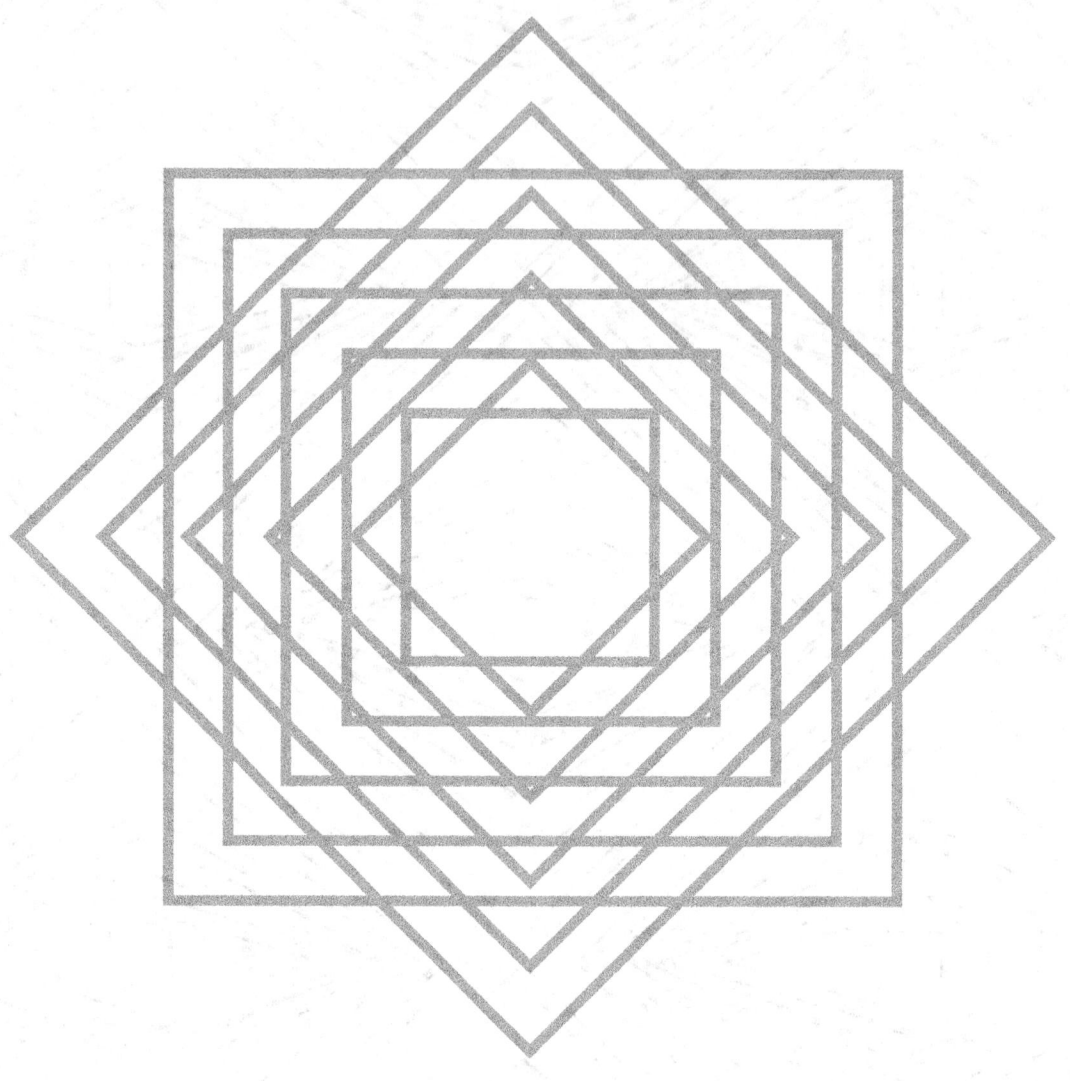

pattern # 14

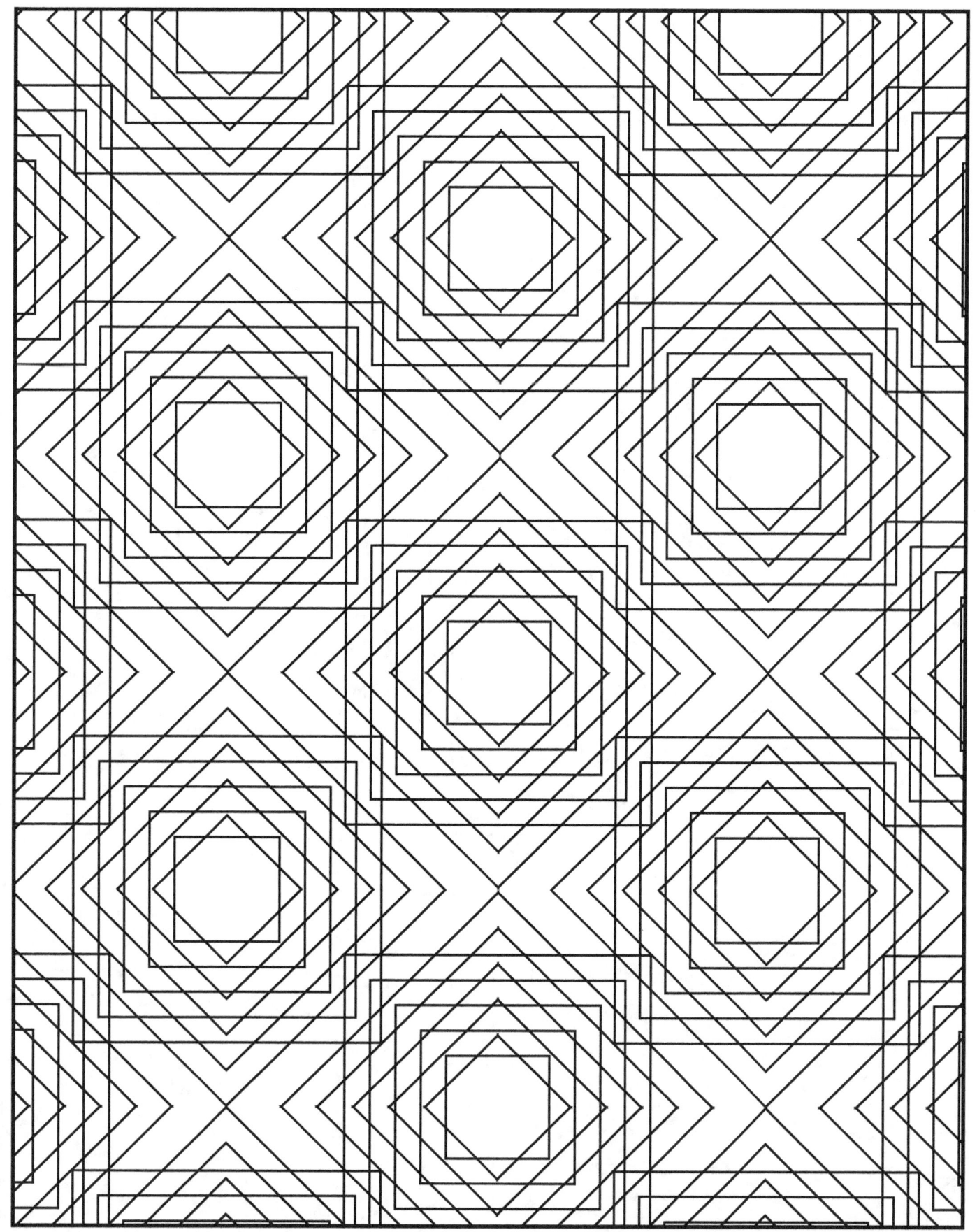

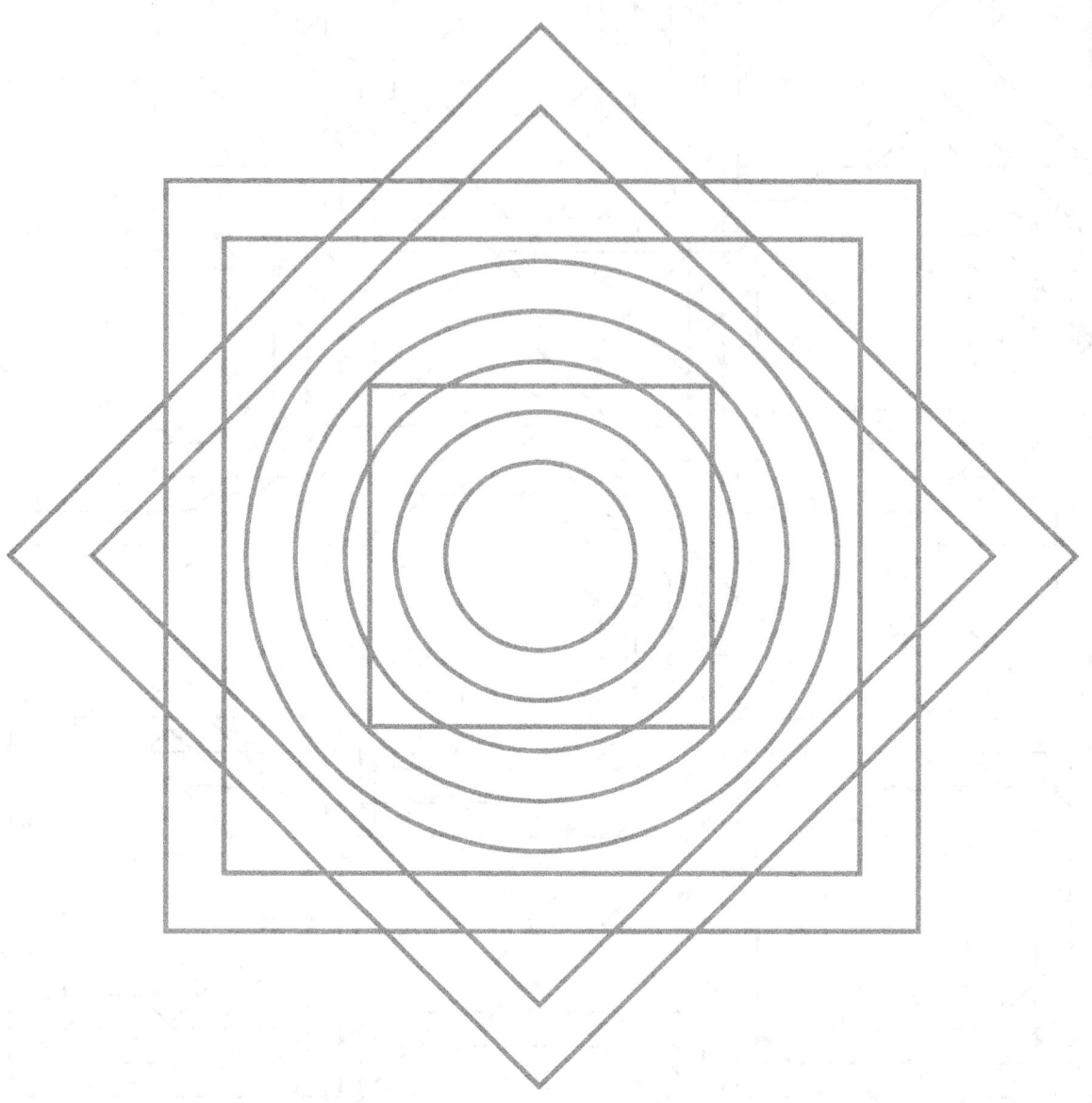

pattern # 15

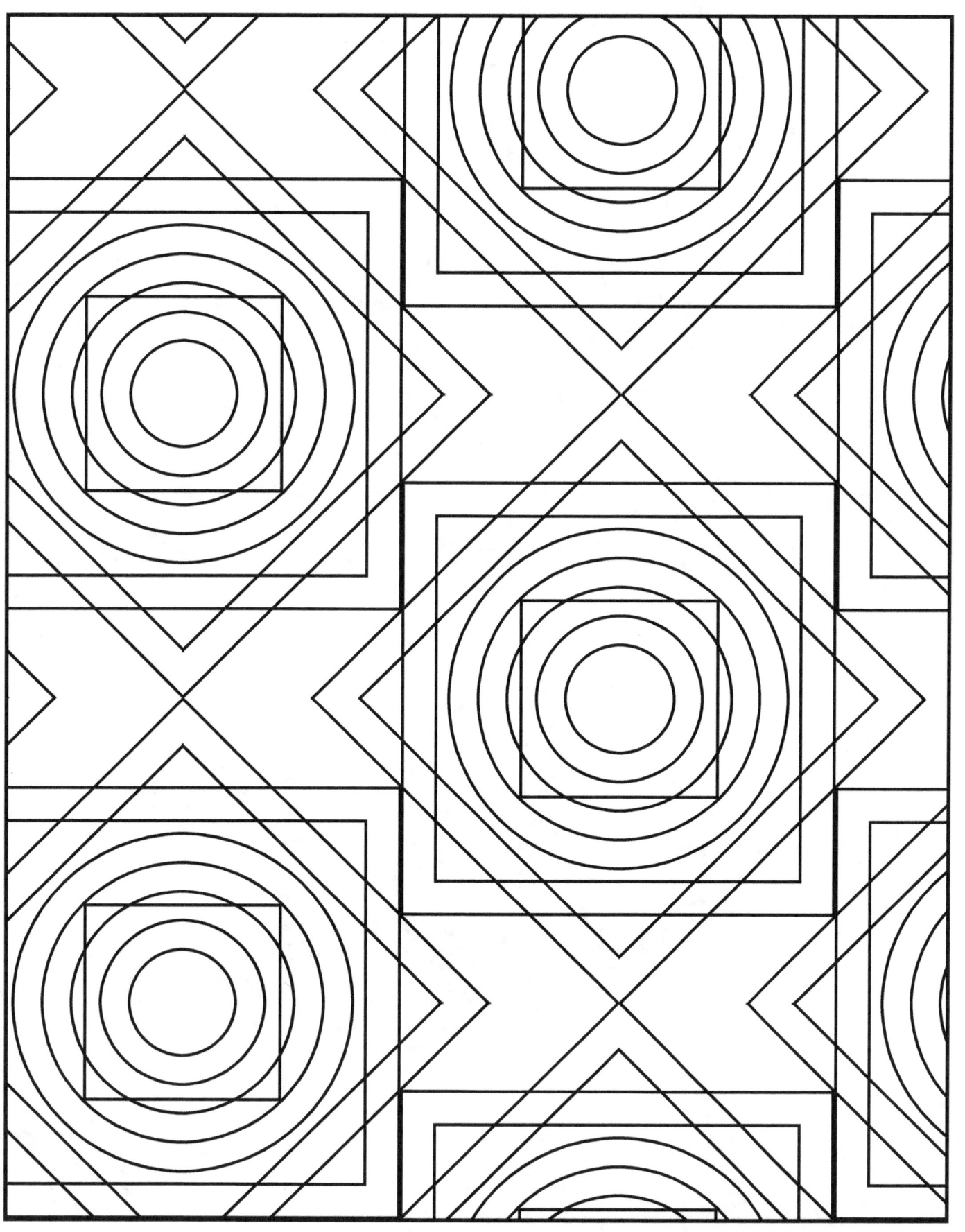

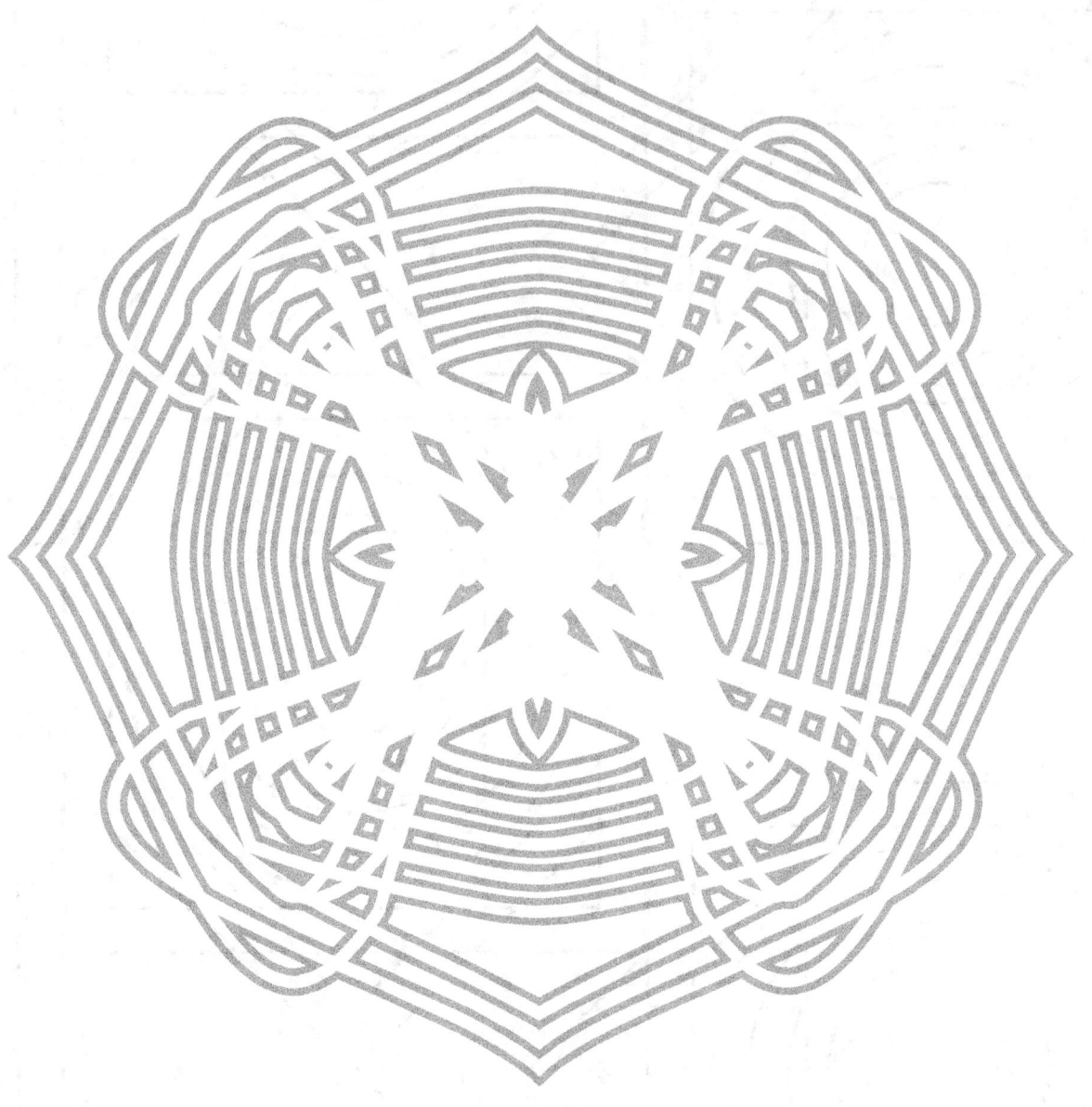

pattern # 16

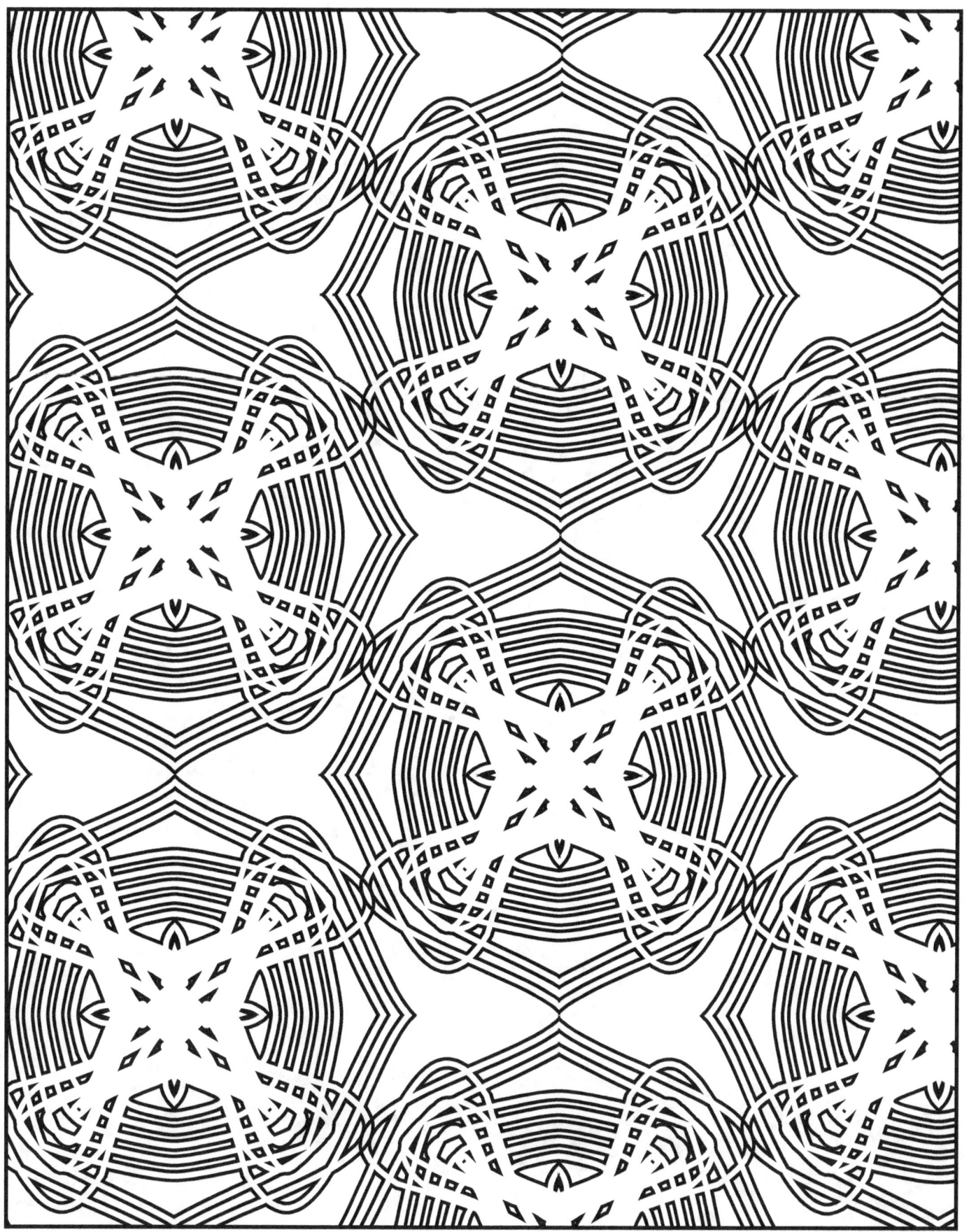

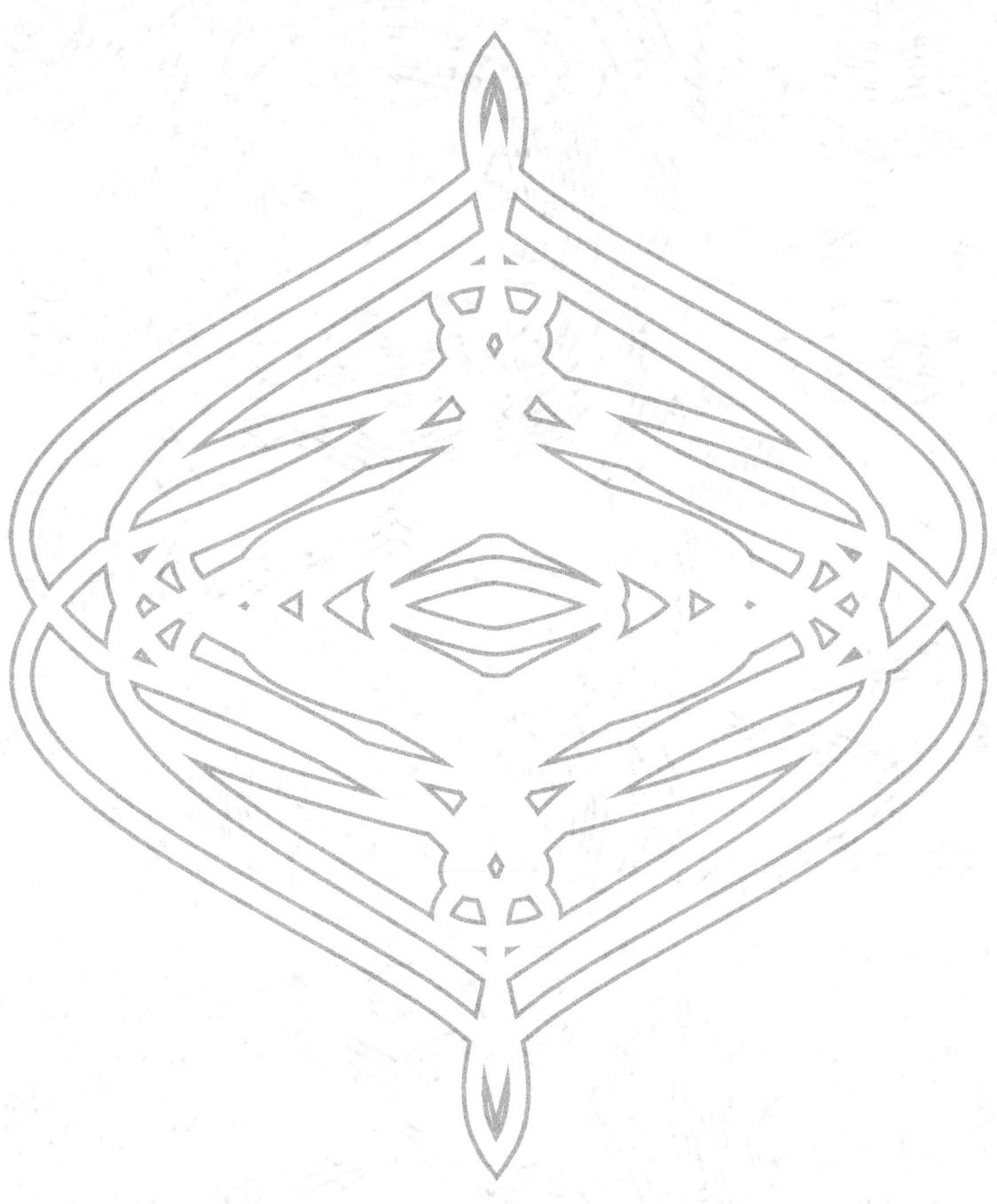

pattern # 17

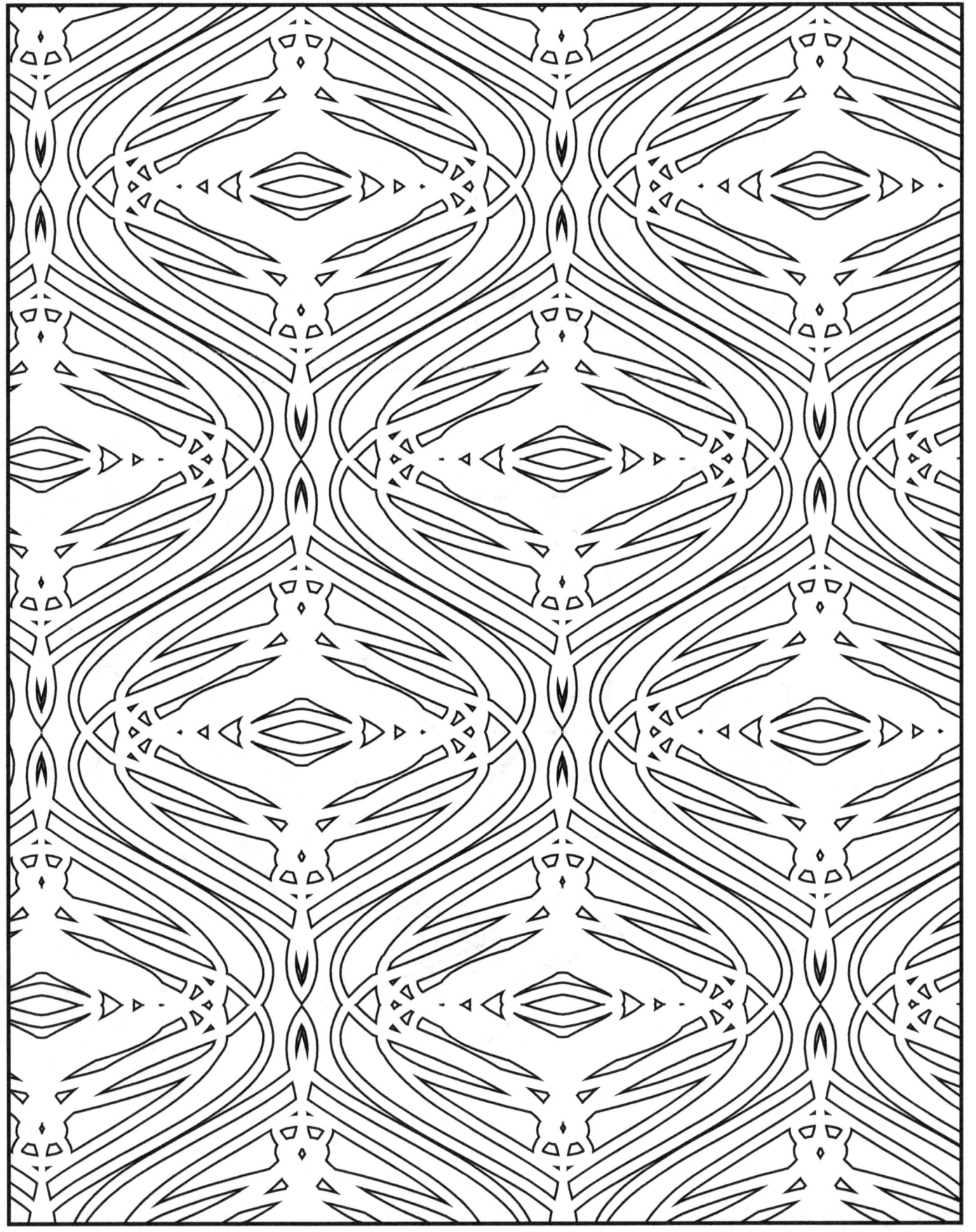

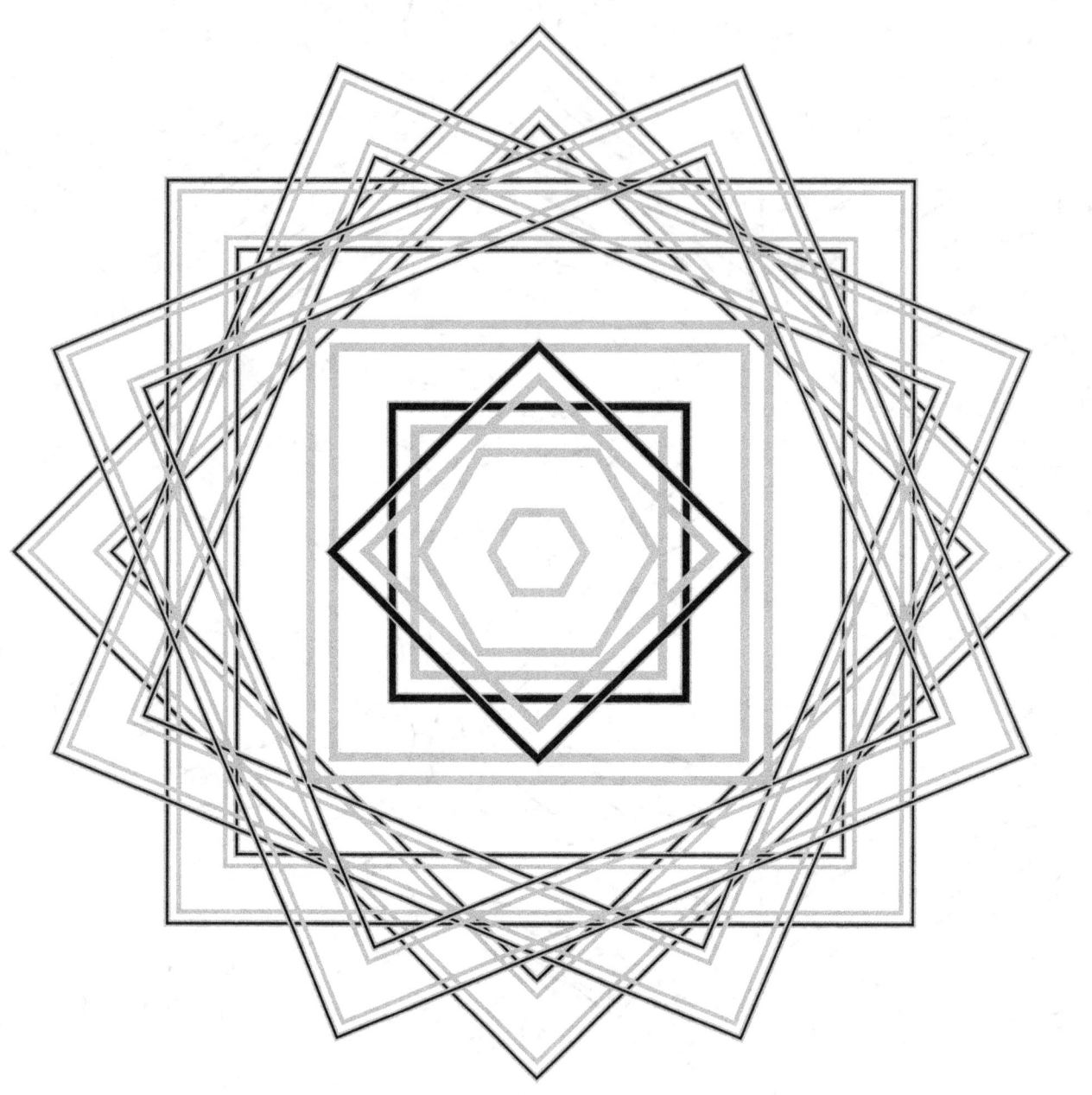

pattern # 18

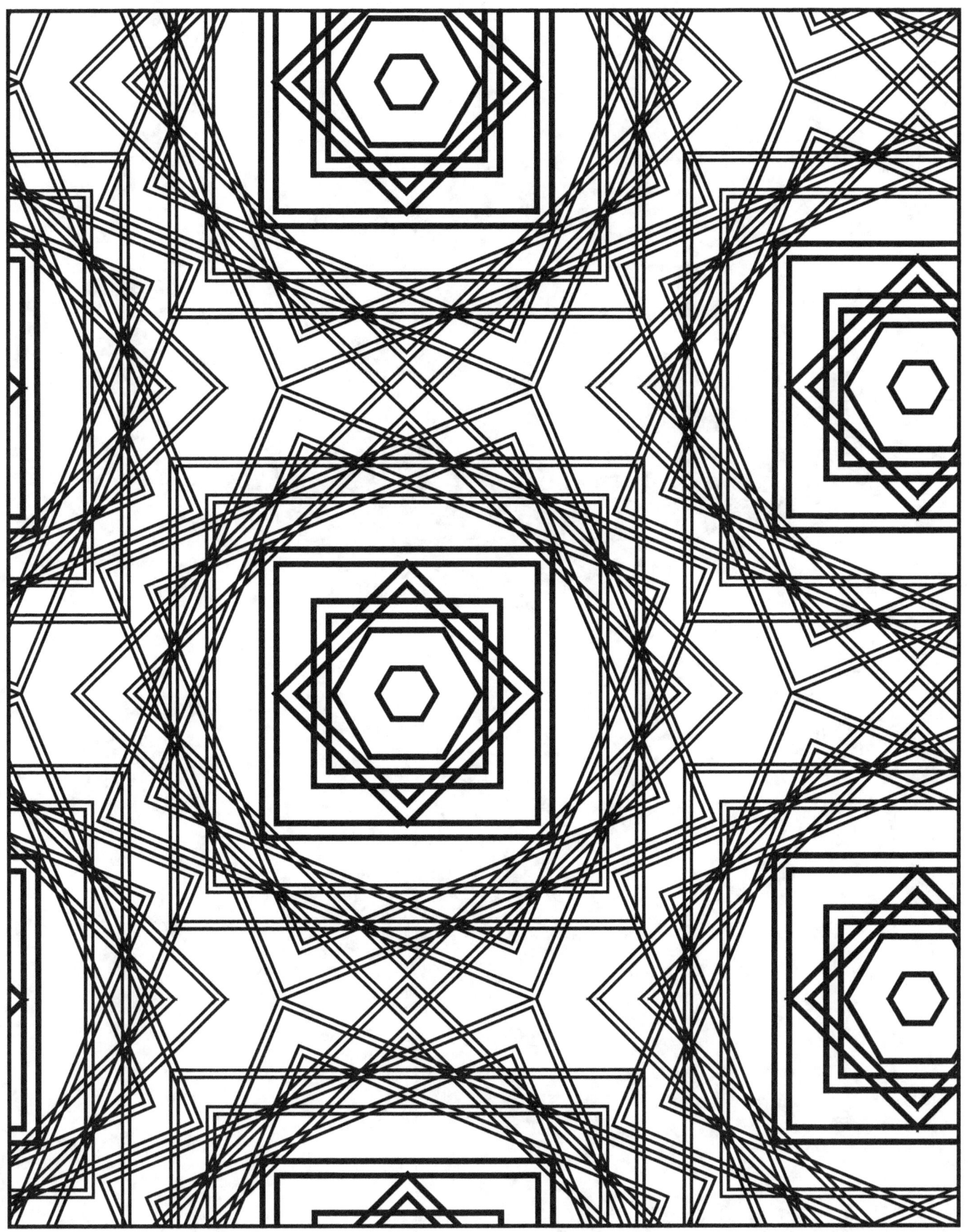

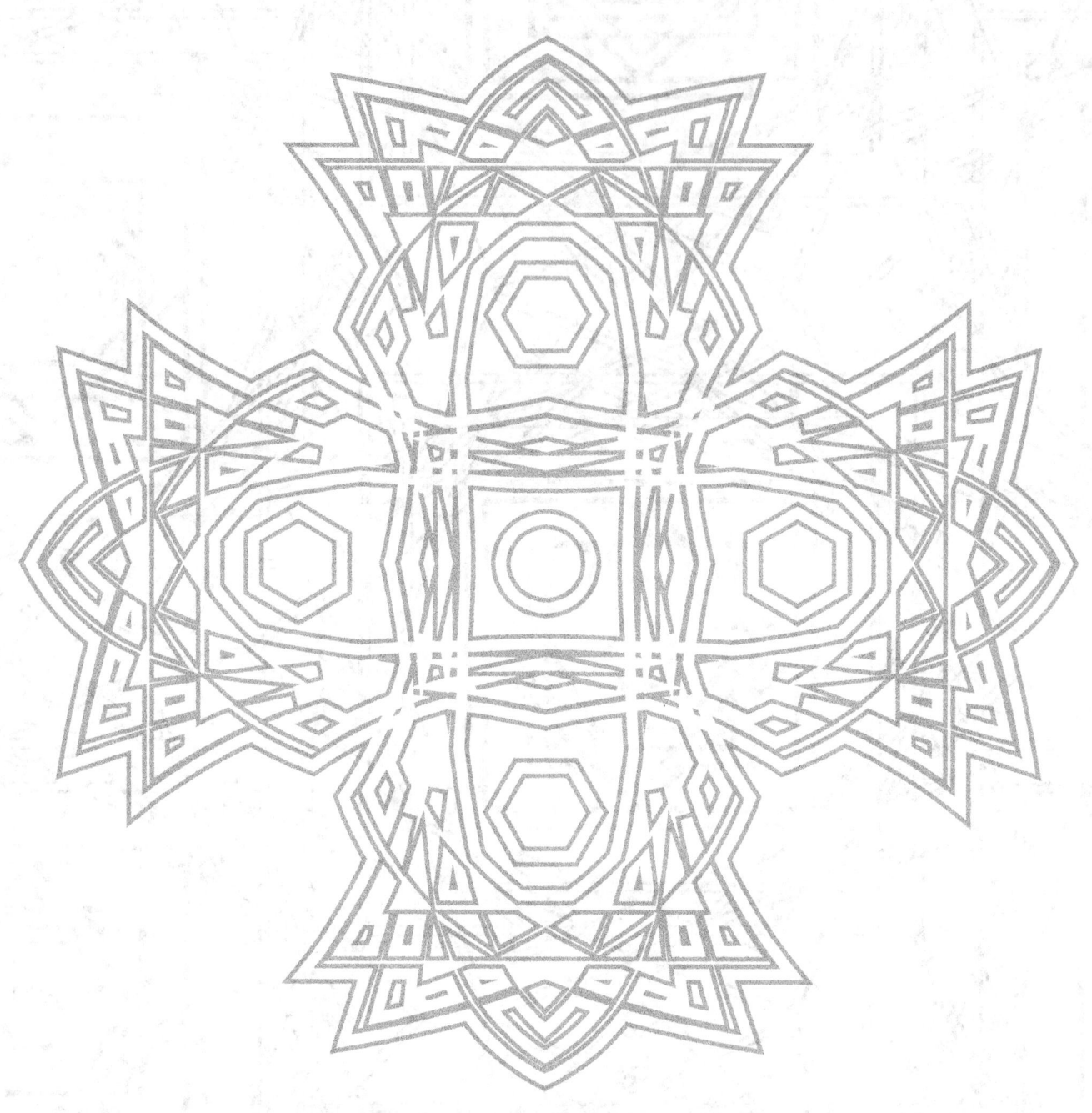

pattern # 19

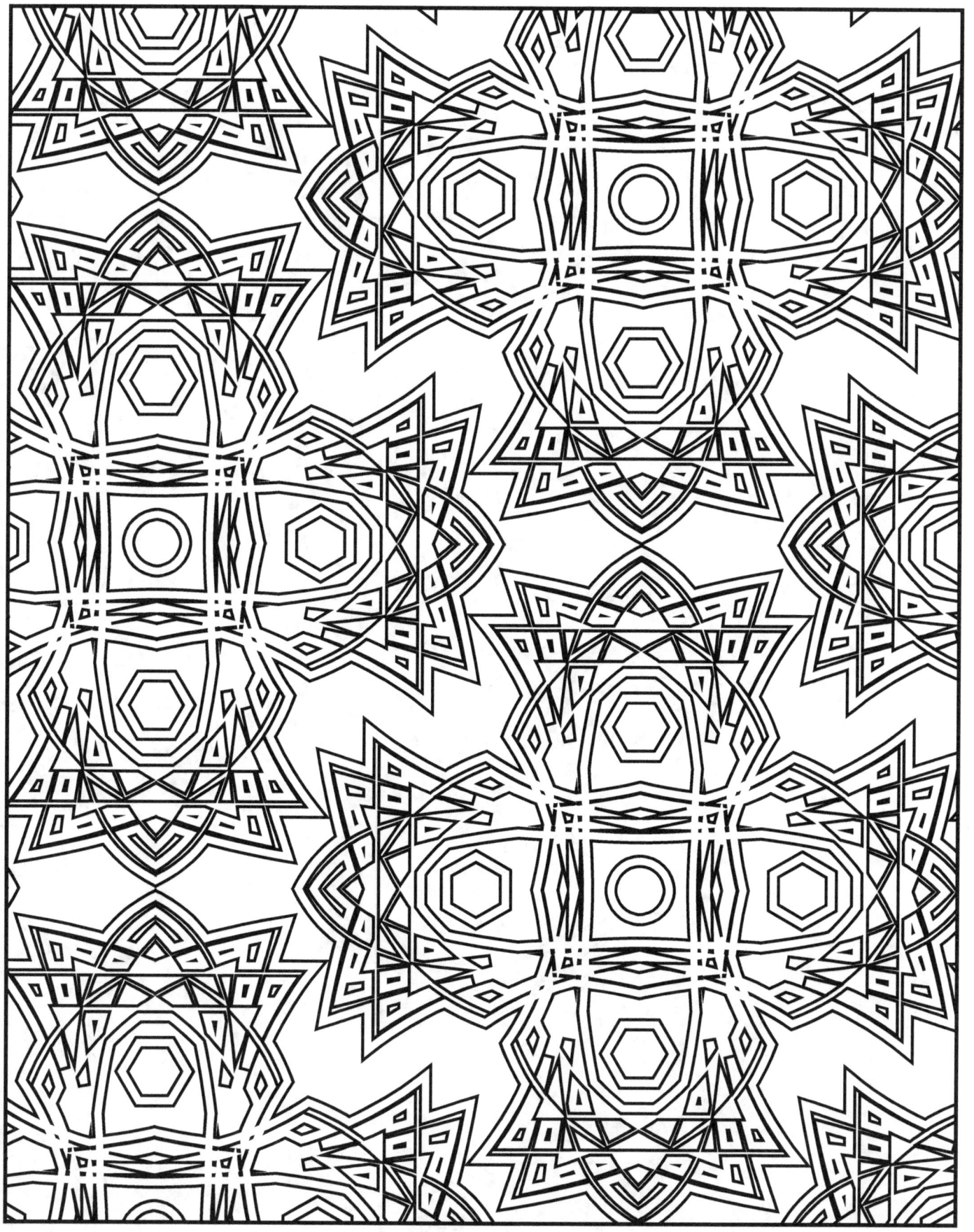

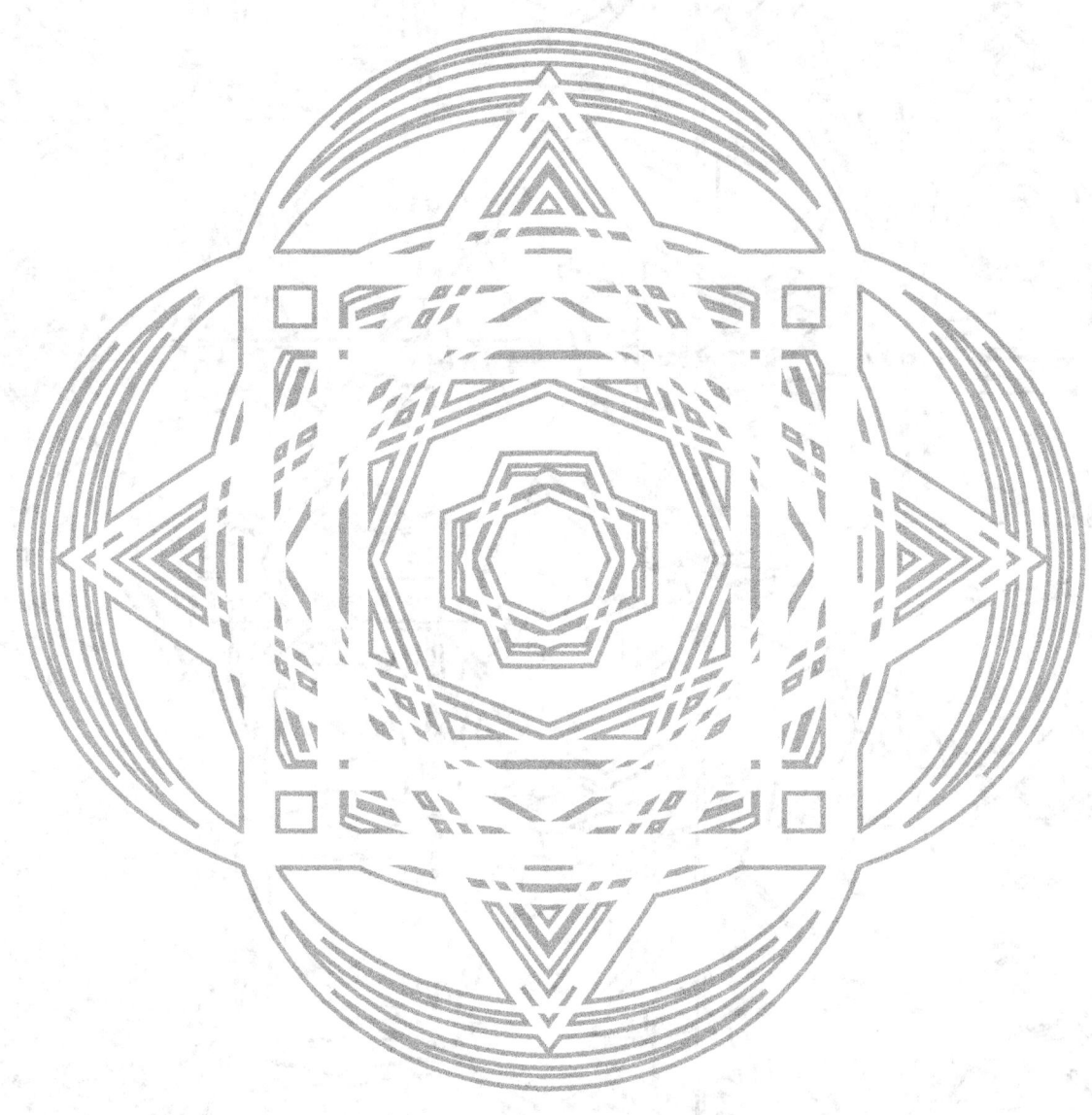

pattern # 20

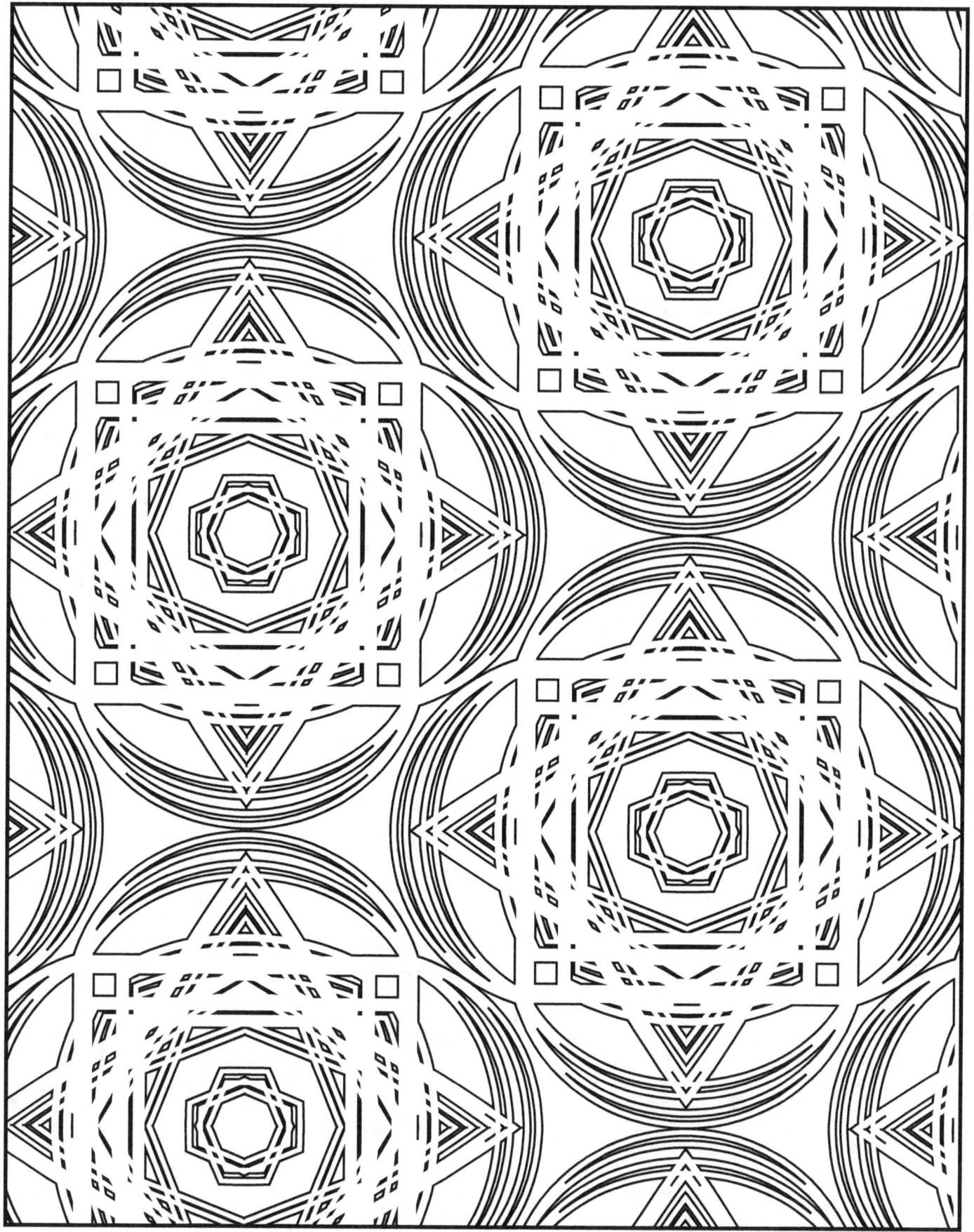

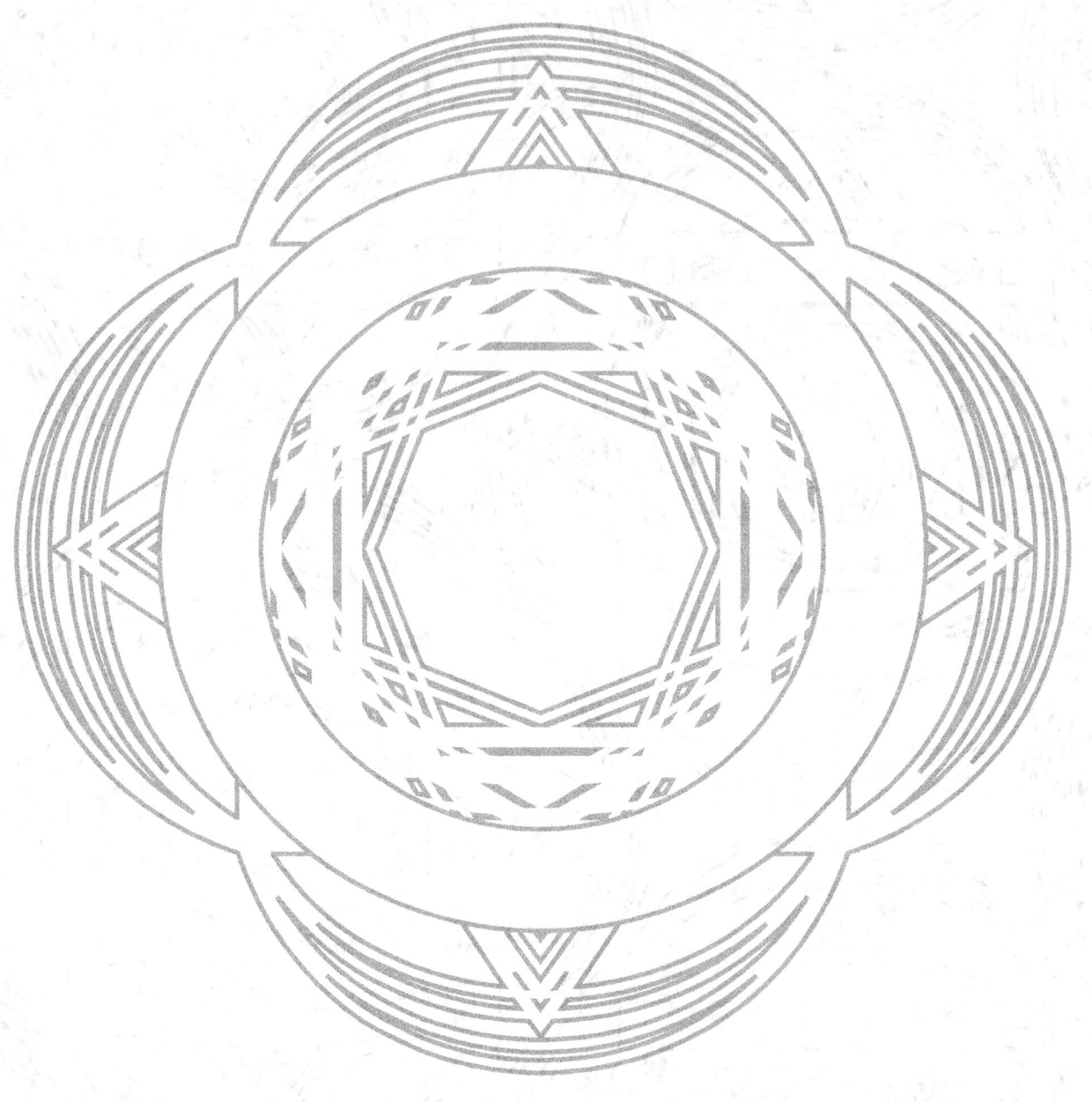

pattern # 21

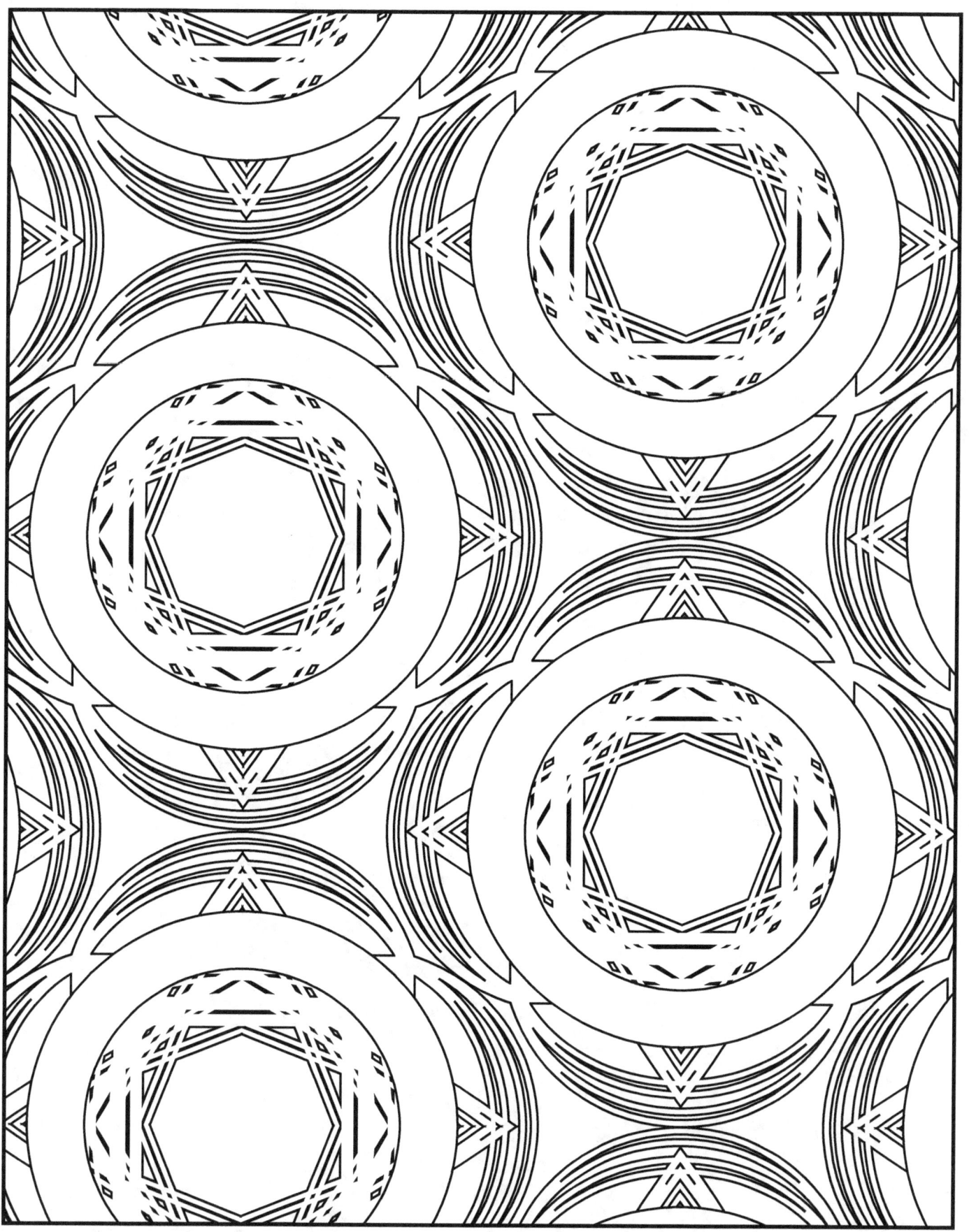

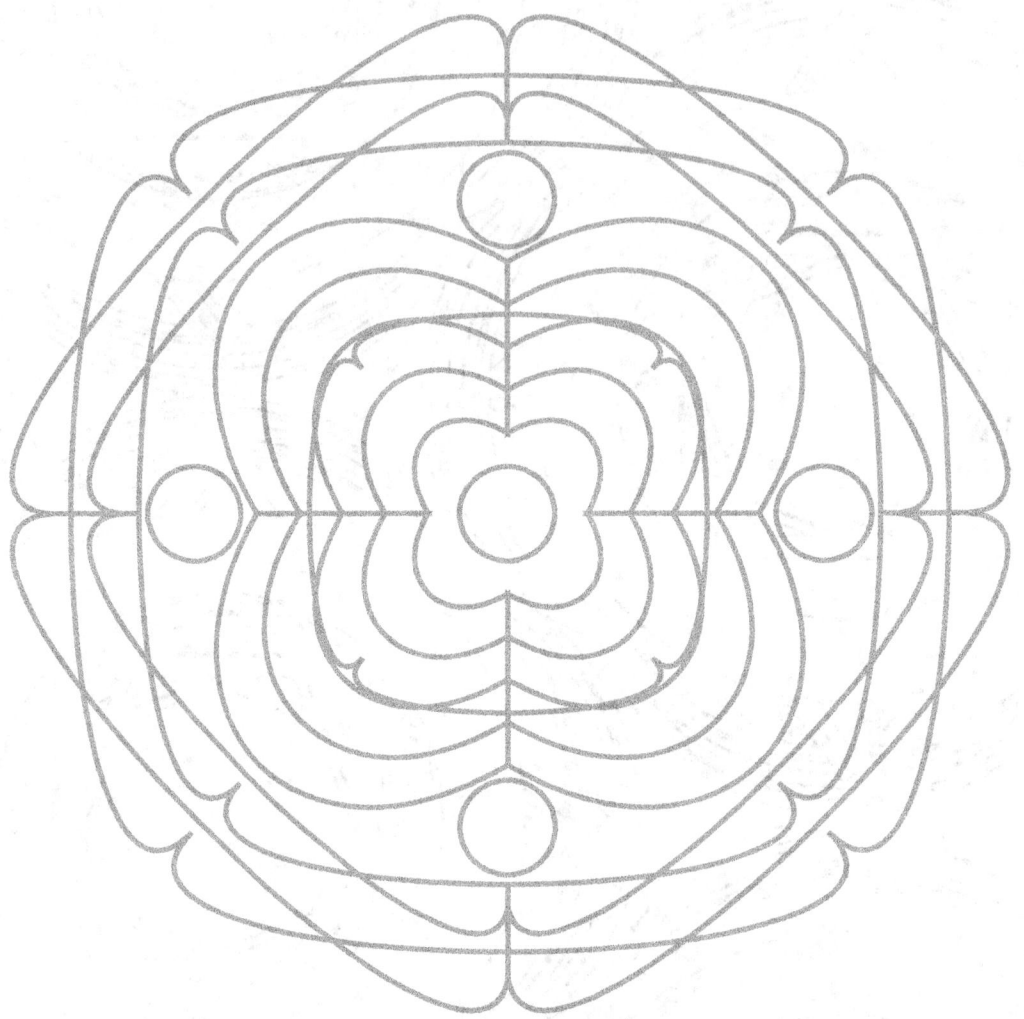

pattern # 22

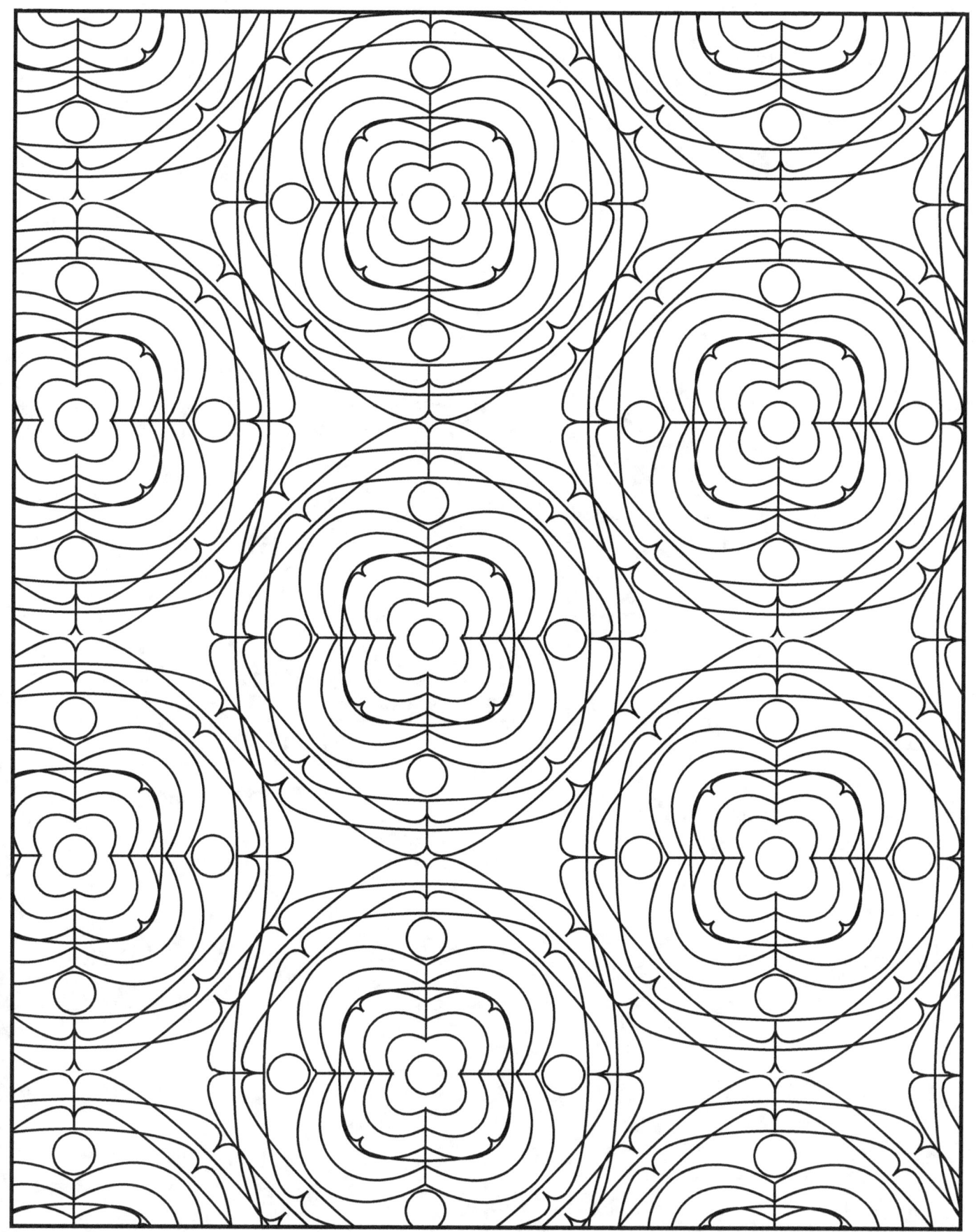

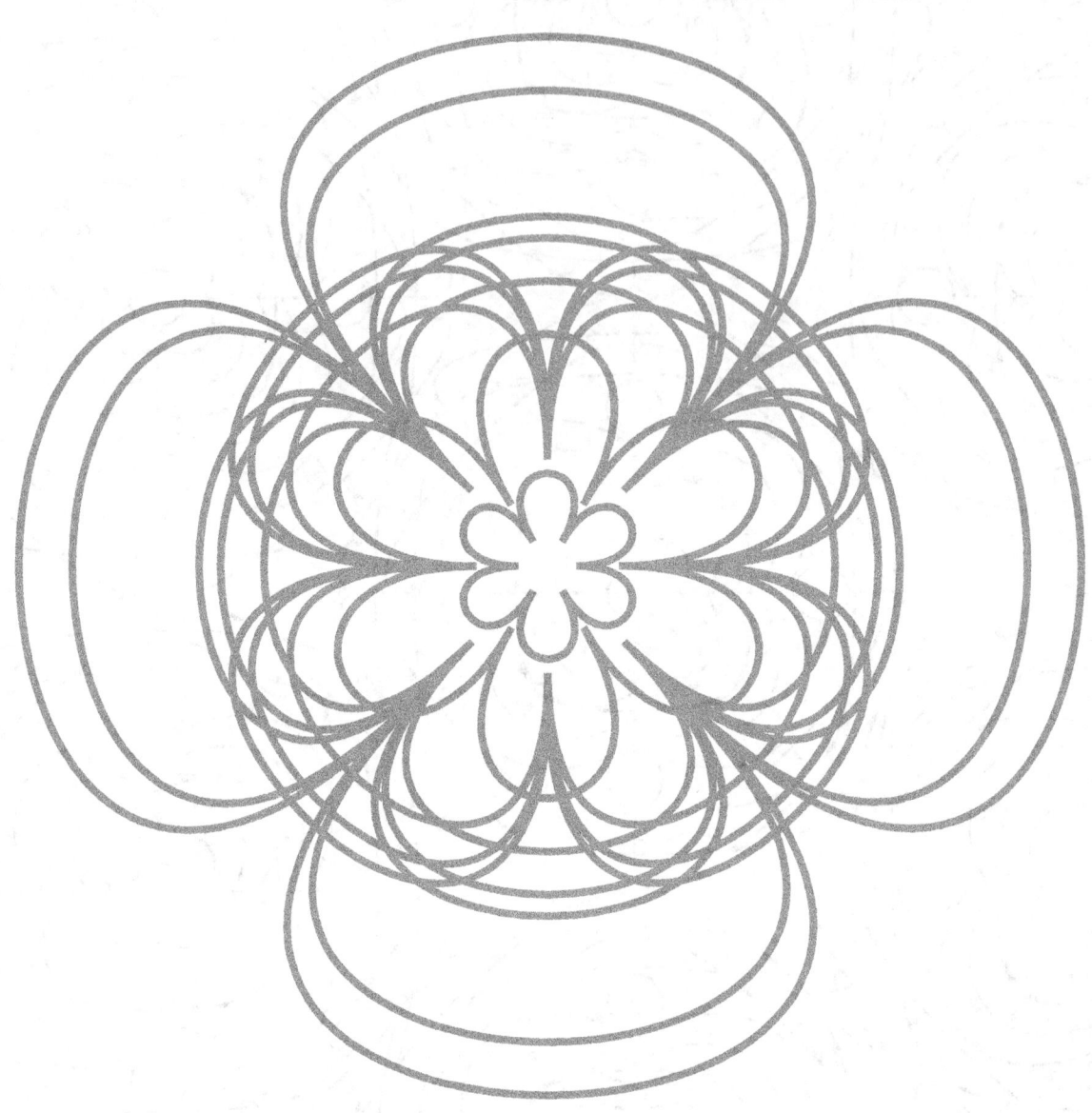

pattern # 23

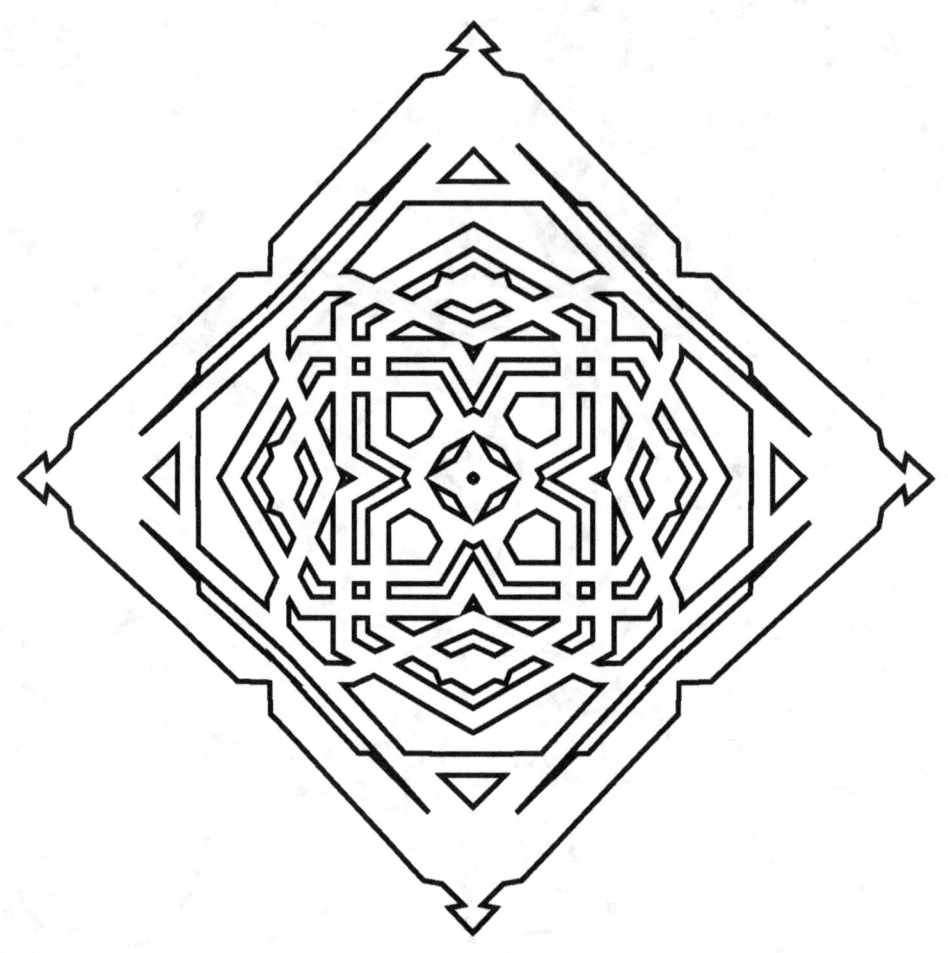

pattern # 24

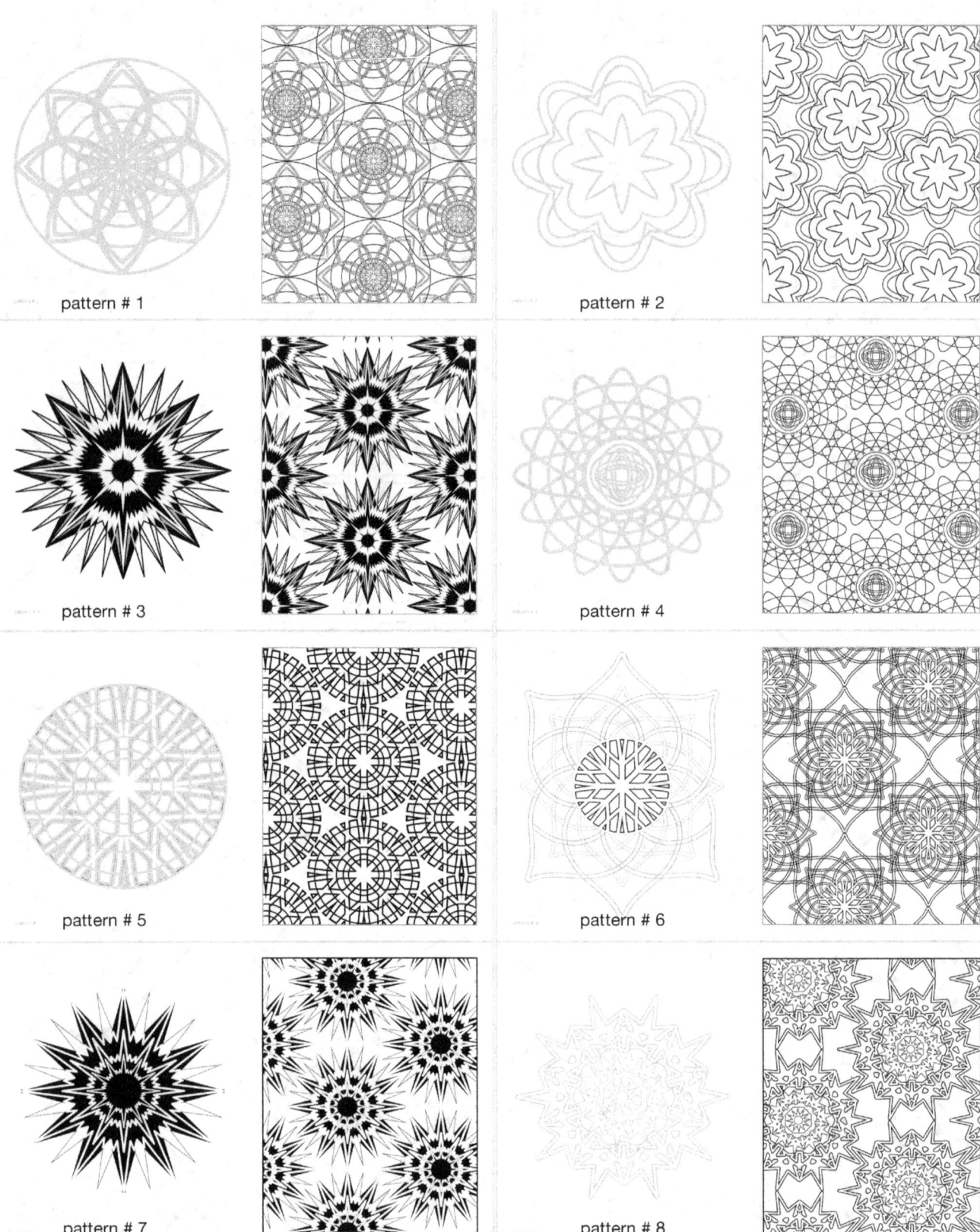

pattern # 1

pattern # 2

pattern # 3

pattern # 4

pattern # 5

pattern # 6

pattern # 7

pattern # 8

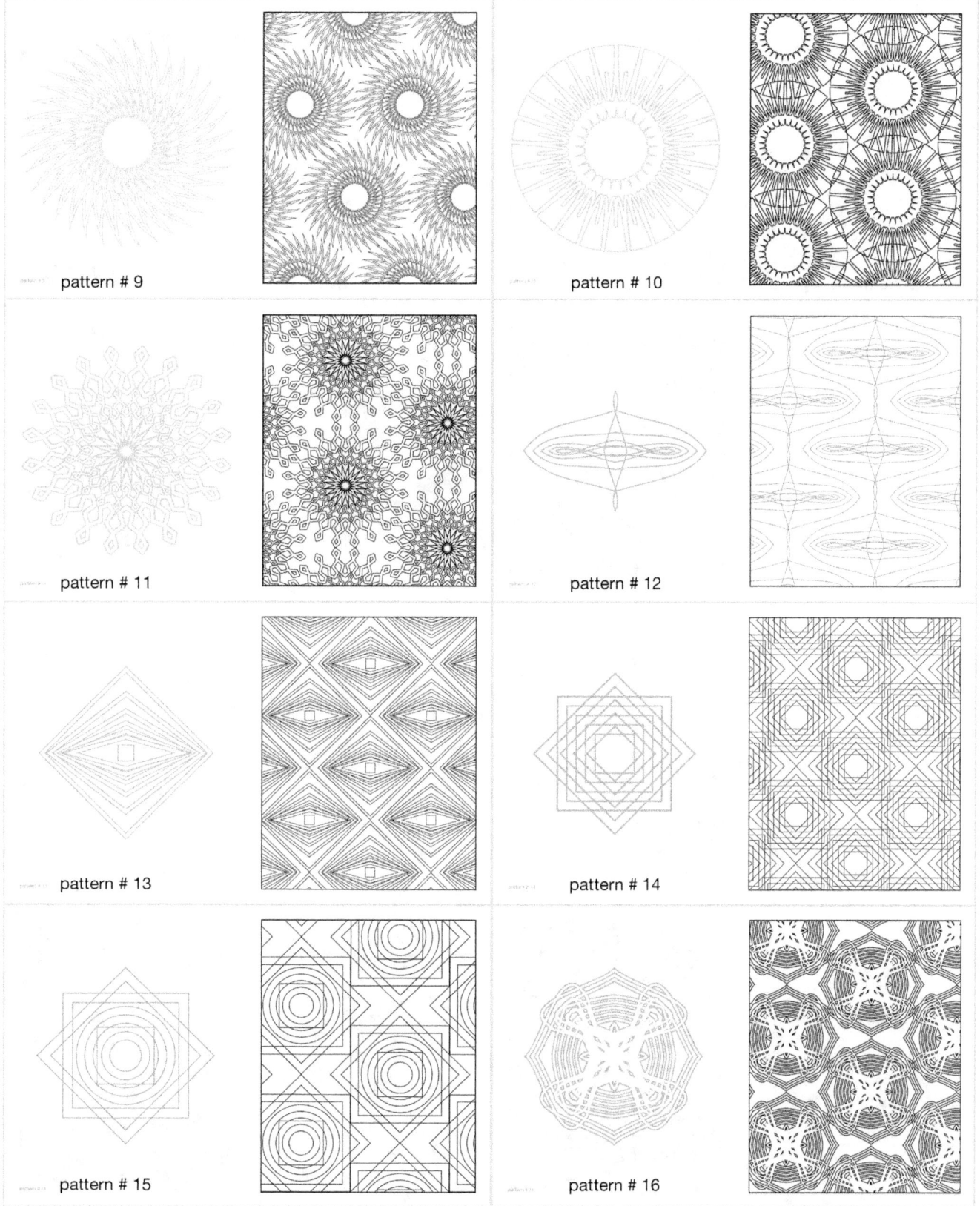

pattern # 9

pattern # 10

pattern # 11

pattern # 12

pattern # 13

pattern # 14

pattern # 15

pattern # 16

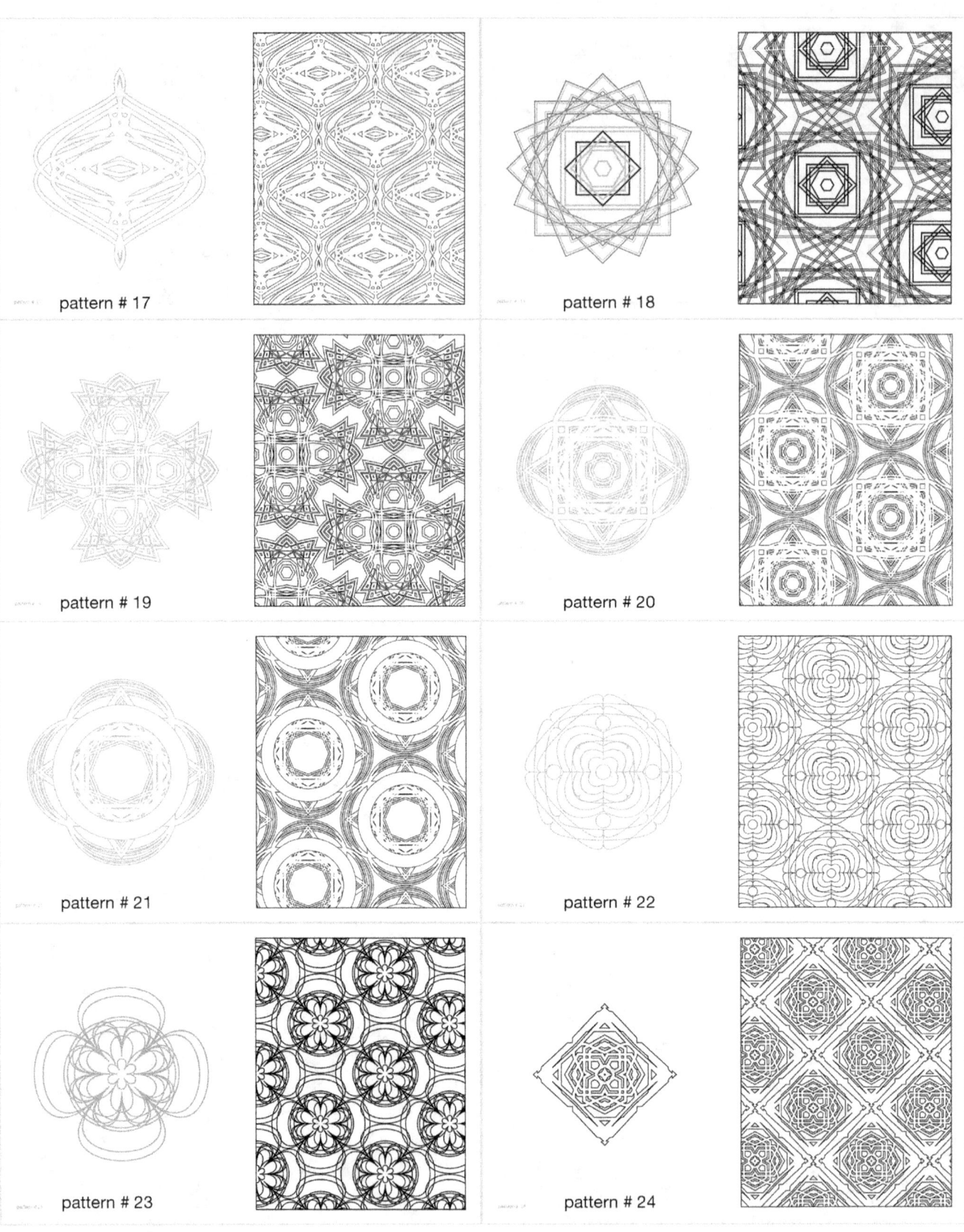

pattern # 17

pattern # 18

pattern # 19

pattern # 20

pattern # 21

pattern # 22

pattern # 23

pattern # 24

Symmetry Masters is a team of professional designers and illustrators that share inspiration with symmetrical structures and pattern design.
All designs by the Symmetry Masters are unique computer generated artwork turned in to repeated patterns.

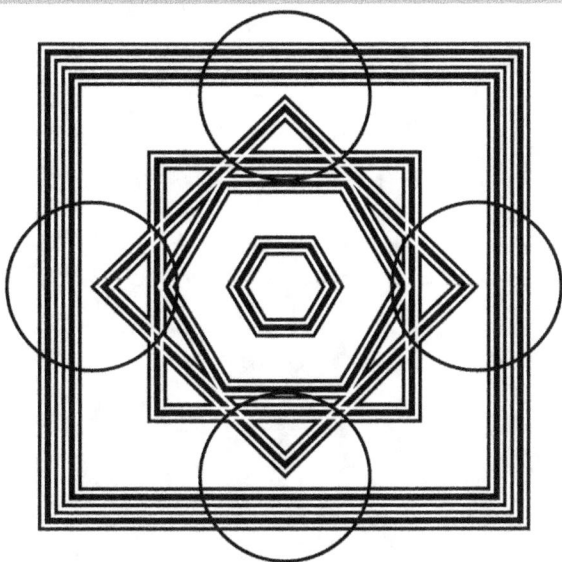

Designs created for coloring or creative inspiration. Have fun uncovering element depicted to the left in the pattern shown to the right.

Get creative ideas for your professional or hobby project exploring symmetrical styles and pattern arrangements.
Collection of design elements in the book ranges from very simple to complex and sophisticated artwork.
Select your challenge, pick you inspiration!

Symmetry is a beautiful marvel.

Let us enjoy some order in this chaotic life!!!

48 designs for color and inspiration
24 symmetrical design elements + 24 patterns
by
The Symmetry Masters